American Alligator

The "gator" is certainly Florida's most famous animal. It is the mascot for the University of Florida and is depicted on many Florida souvenirs. Even the gator's name is entwined with the state's history. The earliest European explorers in Florida were from Spain. They called this strange and previously unknown creature "el lagarto," which means "the lizard" in Spanish. English sailors and settlers later corrupted "el lagarto" into "allagarto" or "allagarter."

The gator is an ancient animal that has survived from the age of the dinosaurs. It is found only in the southeastern United States, from North Carolina to Texas. The only other species of alligator in the world is found in China, but it is smaller and quite rare.

Gators were once incredibly abundant in Florida. Although their population now is only a fraction of what it was 150 years ago, they are still found all over the state in fresh-water lakes, ponds, rivers, roadside ditches, and throughout the Everglades where they seek refuge during the dry season in so-called "gator holes."

Alligator mississippiensis. SPECIES OF SPECIAL CONCERN. *Range in Florida: entire state in fresh water. Maximum length: 16 feet.*

THE MEANING OF RANGE

In this book, "range" refers to range in Florida. Many of the creatures described have ranges which extend well beyond Florida's borders.

WHAT IS COVERED

This book deals with Florida's most conspicuous and fascinating reptiles and amphibians. It includes almost all of the species found in the state, omitting the few that are unlikely to ever be seen by the average person. Most of the animals described are found in the southern two-thirds of the peninsula. Also included are some of the unique or very famous species found in the panhandle or the northeastern part of the state, such as the Alligator Snapping Turtle, Pine Barrens Treefrog, Florida Bog Frog, Gray Treefrog, Canebrake Rattlesnake, Southern Copperhead, and the Gray Rat Snake.

△ This gator seems to be basking in peaceful coexistence with its turtle neighbors. Some turtles are large enough and have shells strong enough to resist a gator's jaws (depending on the relative sizes of the gator and the turtle). Turtles smaller than the ones shown here probably would not dare to sun themselves right next to this gator.

HERPS

The only English word that refers to both reptiles and amphibians is "herptile" – often shortened to "herp." These terms do not appear in most dictionaries, but the word "herpetologist" does. Herpeton in Greek means "creeping thing." A herpetologist is a person who specializes in the study of reptiles or amphibians.

HERPS AND THE LAW

Many of Florida's herptiles are rare or are experiencing serious population declines. Habitat destruction, over-collecting, and deliberate or accidental killing have threatened several species with extinction. Florida has enacted laws to help protect certain animals and to ensure the survival of healthy populations. Without a permit from the Florida Game and Fresh Water Fish Commission (FGFWFC), it is illegal to "pursue, molest, harass, capture or possess" any individual, nest, eggs, or parts of herptiles that are designated by the FGFWFC as either ENDANGERED or THREATENED. Offenders that are caught face serious fines and/or imprisonment.

In this book, a third classification is SPECIES OF SPECIAL CONCERN. These species are monitored by the FGFWFC because they are either rare or declining in numbers. Most species in this category, like the alligator, are protected by specific legislation. Species that were classified in any of the above categories as of January 1, 1990, are clearly indicated in this book.

GATOR EXTREMES

The largest gator ever recorded was killed in Louisiana in 1890. It measured 19 feet, 2 inches. How old do gators get? Despite many fanciful tales, the average lifespan of an alligator is about 40 years in the wild and 50 in captivity. Record life spans are perhaps ten years longer.

How long can an alligator hold its breath and stay underwater? If a gator is cruising around slowly and submerges simply to disappear or to rest beneath the water, it can remain there from one to several hours, provided it stays still or moves slowly. With vigorous underwater exercise, however, the gator needs to surface more often in order to breathe. Gator wrestlers have sometimes unintentionally drowned gators by holding them underwater, only briefly, while they were energetically thrashing around.

THE TIP OF THE ICEBERG

When a gator is swimming on the surface, only its head and part of its back protrude above the water. While in this comfortable position, however, it can breathe, see, hear, smell and taste.

A gator swims with its legs tucked against its body, moving forward quietly by sweeping its powerful tail from side to side. While swimming on the surface of the water, it can often approach its prey without being noticed because it so closely resembles a floating log.

ALLIGATOR

The yellow bands on these baby gators will disappear as they mature.

Alligator courtship takes place in the spring. In Florida, it usually begins around the first part of April. Wild female gators begin reproducing at eight to ten years of age, captive ones at about six years. Recent studies have shown that gators (and crocodiles) have a very keen sense of smell. Two glands near the base of the tail emit scents that can be detected by other gators. These scents are important in locating and attracting mates. Male gators sometimes fight over females but for the most part are tolerant of each other during the mating season.

A male usually mates with only one female during the season. Once the female has selected her partner, he follows her closely for several days. The pair eventually comes to rest in a suitable place in shallow water. The male lies beside the female for some time and occasionally strokes her back. When she is sufficiently aroused, copulation takes place.

About two months after mating, the female builds her nest. She does this by scraping together a mound of earth and plant debris about 2 to 3 feet high. Her nest may be located in direct sunlight or in the shade of trees. It is usually about 10 to 15 feet from water. The female gator uses a hind foot to dig a cavity into the top of the nest. When she is ready, she straddles the nest and lays between 30 and 50 eggs in the cavity, using her hind feet to break the fall of the eggs.

Alligator eggs are usually laid at night. They have a hard, whitish shell. After the eggs are laid, the female moves gingerly over the sides of the nest until the top of the cavity is closed by the pressure of her weight. Humidity in the nest is always high, and the fermenting plant material of which the nest is made helps keep the temperature at the proper level for incubation. Certain turtle species take advantage of these features by laying their eggs in alligator nest mounds.

△ Baby gators can be more than a handful as these eager little fellows prove (and they are not too small to bite!). Hatchling gators usually stick together for the first year or two, and these small groups are called "pods." One possible benefit of banding together is that the group has more eyes with which to watch for predators such as birds and raccoons.

△ The female gator guards her nest carefully, spending many hours resting with her chin on top of it. If an animal or human intruder approaches, she turns to face the threat, hisses, and lunges with an open mouth if the intruder comes too close. The female stays on or very near the nest until the young are hatched. It is definitely advisable to avoid approaching a female that is guarding a nest.

HEAT AND GENDER

In the early 1980s, a fascinating fact came to light. Alligators and crocodiles (and most turtles) lack sex chromosomes. The sex of these creatures is actually determined by the temperature at which their eggs incubate. This phenomenon is called TSD (for temperature-dependent sex determination). In an alligator nest, the eggs that incubate between 90° and 93°F become males, while those incubating between 82° and 86°F become females. From 87° to 89°, the ratio of males to females is about equal. Since the eggs at the top of the gator's nest are likely to be heated more by the sun than those below, males usually come from the top part of the nest while females come from the bottom. On the contrary, with crocodiles, females come from the warmest eggs.

In artificial breeding programs, the ratio of males to females can easily be controlled by regulating the temperature of the incubating eggs. Some farms incubate most of their eggs at 90°F or higher to obtain males, since males grow bigger.

One theory explaining the disappearance of the dinosaurs is that the cooling of the earth changed the sex ratio of dinosaurs, producing either all males or all females.

△ Broods of baby gators hatch from mid August through September. Although hatchlings sometimes climb out of the nest alone, they are usually assisted by the mother. She is normally alerted by the yelping of her babies and clears the top of the nest to help them emerge.

Baby gators are about 8 or 9 inches long upon hatching and beautifully marked with yellow and black bands. As soon as they are free from the nest, they head straight for the water, usually further assisted and guarded by their mother.

In captivity, gators add about one foot to their length each year, maybe slightly more, until they are seven or eight years old. Gators in in the wild do not grow as fast, and a three-footer is more likely four to six years of age. The older an alligator becomes, the less it grows each year, and eventually it stops growing altogether. Under ideal conditions, male alligators could grow to a length of about 16 feet, females to about 10 feet.

△ Gators are stealthy, "sit-and-wait" predators. While this gator was in the water, the duckweed (a common native plant which grows on the surface of ponds) was part of his camouflage. On dry land, this gator is still a bit green in the face.

GATOR EYES AT NIGHT

A powerful flashlight scanning the surface of a quiet pond at night often reveals a glow from the eyes of a floating gator. This is a tactic that hide hunters have used for decades to locate their victims. Although some people claim that the glow from the eyes of females and young is greenish or yellowish, most authorities maintain that the glow is red for all gators regardless of sex or age. The green or yellowish eyeshine sometimes seen at night in gator habitat usually comes from the eyes of bullfrogs, pig frogs or water spiders that float on the surface. Water spiders can be as large as 4 or 5 inches across and their eyes are highly reflective, so it is not too surprising that their eyes are sometimes mistaken for those of a small gator.

A gator's eyes are no less interesting than other parts of its anatomy. The eyes sit well back on the top of the head so that they can take in a wide field of view. Gators have excellent vision, even at night. Their eyes have two sets of eyelids. The outer set closes like ours, from top to bottom. The inner eyelid, called the "nictitating membrane," closes from rear to front and is transparent. This membrane covers and protects the sensitive eyeball like built-in goggles, permitting the gator to see clearly underwater.

ALLIGATOR

The "Water Dance"

GATOR VIBES

One of the gator's most conspicuous habits is its loud bellowing. Contrary to popular belief, it is not just the males that bellow, and apparently bellowing is not related to mating, since most of it occurs after the female has already laid her eggs. Bellowing is done by both males and females, by night and day, from the water and from land, and may occur at any time during the creatures' active period, which is usually the warmer months of the year. Bellowing is not a sign of hostility but seems to be simply a means by which gators announce their presence to one another. Certain natural or man-made noises, such as thunder, loud music, or the sound of a truck or tractor can stimulate gators to bellow.

Just before a male gator bellows audibly, its whole torso vibrates. If it is floating on the surface of the water, sprays of fine water droplets dance off its back like they would from a vibrating tuning fork dipped into water. This unique phenomenon has been called the gator's "water dance."

△▽ The male gator's social display: (A) The lifting of the head and tail. (B) Posturing, raising the body out of the water to demonstrate size. (C) Audible bellowing plus the water dance. The water dance is accompanied by "infrasound," notes too low for the human ear but which travel long distances and can be heard by other gators.

THE SKIN TRADE

Alligator hide products crafted by big-name European designers fetch high prices. In Hong Kong, alligator purses now sell for as much as $3,000 and briefcases for $7,000. It is not hard to see why the alligator was nearly hunted to extinction if the handsome, hide of its belly can be made into products that sell for these prices. It is officially estimated that over ten million gators were killed in Florida between 1870 and 1970! Although larger specimens have always been preferred by hide hunters, young gators were also frequently killed for the edible flesh of their tails.

The killing of alligators for their attractive skins led to such severe population declines that gator hunting in Florida was banned in 1961. Poaching, however, continued until effective federal laws were passed in the late 1960s to control the companies that were processing and selling hides and to ban interstate trade in illegal hides. These laws served to curtail the slaughter and to prevent the total disappearance of gators in the wild. When gator populations had increased substantially, hunting was again permitted on a limited basis. Fortunately, the gator is a durable creature whose population has recovered

substantially after it was protected by law.

At present, the collecting or killing of alligators is strictly regulated by Florida laws. Hunters can obtain permits only through an annual drawing, after which winners are informed where they may hunt and how many gators they may "harvest." Application pro-

◁ After alligator hides are dyed, a high-gloss finish is produced by brushing on a glaze and then rolling the surface under heavy pressure with a small glass cylinder.

Why should an alligator purse cost thousands of dollars when you can buy the whole gator (and a fairly large one) from a hunter for a few hundred dollars? There are several reasons for the high price of alligator products. First, the processing of the leather is a lengthy procedure requiring 15 to 20 steps and a lot of hand labor. Second, the hides pass from hunters or alligator farms to hide-buyers, then to exporters, tanneries, designers/manufacturers, importers, and finally to the retail boutiques with the price marked up, and sometimes doubled, every step of the way. Finally, the addition of famous designer labels pushes the price even higher.

cedures are handled by the Florida Game and Fresh Water Fish Commission.

In 1989, according to the FGFWFC, 207 hunters harvested 3,118 gators. The average length was 7 feet. Depending upon the quality, the market price of raw hides ranged from about $40 to $50 per foot.

GATOR WRESTLING

How do showmen wrestle large alligators without getting bitten? First of all, an alligator's jaw muscles are designed primarily for closing the jaws, not for opening them. It takes very little pressure to keep the jaws of a gator clamped shut, though the biting power of a gator has been measured at 3,000 pounds per square inch! The first rule in gator wrestling is to grab the animal's snout quickly, hold its jaws together, and don't let go! Also, if a gator can be flipped on its back, the flow of blood to the brain is impeded and the animal suddenly becomes immobile, almost as if it has fainted. Gator wrestlers make use of this weakness. In a strictly show-biz stunt, they pretend to put the creature to sleep by rubbing its belly while it is lying motionless on its back. All of these tactics work satisfactorily with small-to-medium-sized gators. Gator wrestlers avoid tackling the really big ones, those longer than eight feet.

GATOR DENS

During its inactive period in the colder months of the year, a gator can stay beneath the water for a considerable length of time, even days. Gators often dig dens and "hole up" along the banks of rivers and lakes during the colder months.

In the northern parts of the alligator's range, where the surfaces of ponds and rivers freeze over during the winter, gators have sometimes been found completely immobile with their snouts protruding upward through the ice.

△ Alligator emerging from its den made of grasses in the Everglades.

△ Alligator den dug into muddy bank, near Lake Okeechobee.

ALLIGATOR FLAG

Alligator Flag, also called Arrowroot and Fireflag, is a plant with long, narrow leaves which grow atop long stems and thus resemble flags. Because it grows in the open, around the alligator ponds of the Everglades, it is associated by name with the presence of gators.

THE IMPORTANCE OF "GATOR HOLES"

Winter is the dry season in the Everglades, and water levels fall drastically. The "River of Grass" becomes dry as the knee-deep water disappears. The harsh effect of this seasonal change on the native creatures is softened by the presence of alligators. Gators find natural depressions in the limestone bedrock and clear out the damp mud with their feet and snouts as they wallow down deeper and deeper. In this way, small ponds are formed, typically ten to twenty feet across and a few feet deep. In addition to being moist habitats for gators, these pondlets provide life-giving water for a variety of animals, including shrimp, small fish, snails, turtles, snakes and frogs. The presence of these aquatic creatures attracts many waterbirds which come to feed, as well as raccoons, otters and bobcats that also visit the holes in search of drinking water. No doubt the gators gobble up a few of these uninvited guests, but most coexist with the gators and thus survive the dry season.

Gators wander during the wet season, but they often return to the same holes in winter, cleaning them out to prevent them from silting up. Gators are thus a vital link in the life cycle of the Everglades. Gator holes have been compared to the oasis water holes found on the plains of Africa, as they bring both predators and prey together in search of life-giving water.

GATORS IN SWIMMING POOLS

During their mating seasons and during droughts, gators often wander extensively. Most wandering gators are three-to-four footers that have gotten too large for their mother's territory and are looking for a home of their own. If a sizable gator appears in a pond or ditch near a home, or perhaps in a swimming pool, and is cause for concern, the Florida Game and Fresh Water Fish Commission will send officers to move the gator to a wilderness location.

HOW GATORS HELP BIRDS

Alligators prey on mammals such as raccoons and opossums when these animals swim out to feed on birds and eggs at waterbird rookeries. In this manner, they benefit the waterbird populations even though they occasionally eat a bird or two themselves.

▷ Old road sign from the early years of the Alligator Alley toll road between Naples and Ft. Lauderdale. Fast moving cars on this highway have spelled doom for wildlife. Wildlife underpasses were added more recently, when I-75 was completed, to help alleviate this problem.

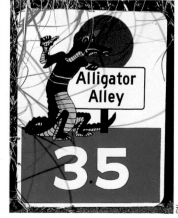

Alligator Alley

3.5

Alligator wallowing in its Everglades "gator hole."

ARE GATORS DANGEROUS TO PEOPLE?

A large gator can be quite dangerous if molested or fed so often that it loses its fear of humans. Although attacks on humans are rare (gators definitely prefer smaller prey), large alligators have maimed or killed a number of careless swimmers and have attacked wading fishermen. Gators are powerful animals and are unpredictable. They should always be given respect. It is dangerous to go swimming in waters known to be inhabited by large gators, particularly at night. Even in daylight, only about one-half of a gator's length is visible while it is swimming.

Alligators do not instinctively attack people without provocation. Generally they are afraid of humans, and in the wild they will usually retreat if a person approaches.

If gators have been living in a body of water where they are not molested and where they see people often, they eventually lose this fear. When people begin feeding such "tame" gators, the animals begin associating humans with food. A big gator that approaches people readily for a handout is dangerous, and hand-feeding such an animal is very risky, since the gator does not distinguish between the food and the hand that is holding it. If a person is swimming in water where a large resident gator is often fed, that gator might approach the swimmer (or a wading fisherman) simply because it expects more food. If the animal is hungry, its primitive feeding instinct might prompt it to grab the luckless human in its powerful jaws.

A female gator that is guarding her nest is especially dangerous, and she is likely to attack anyone who approaches the nest too closely. Nesting females have even been known to attack small boats and to climb aboard airboats in the Everglades.

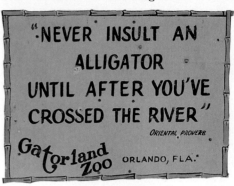

"NEVER INSULT AN ALLIGATOR UNTIL AFTER YOU'VE CROSSED THE RIVER"

ORIENTAL PROVERB

Gatorland Zoo ORLANDO, FLA.

△ This baby egret is a bit too young to fly. The hungry gator is attempting to frighten it or shake it off its perch and into the water, where it would be helpless prey.

JAWS AND TEETH

The massive, heavily-muscled jaws of a large alligator are an awesome sight, especially when the mouth opens to reveal 70 to 80 white, pointed teeth. All of the gator's teeth are similar in shape. They are designed for grasping, holding and crushing. If a gator cannot swallow its prey whole, it pulls, twists and tears at it until gulp-sized chunks are torn off. With large prey such as deer, the gator drags the victim underwater and rolls with it until it drowns. The gator then stashes the body, returning to feed when the flesh has softened through decay. Gators often lose teeth by biting on hard objects, but new teeth grow back as needed, except on older individuals.

A wild alligator's diet includes fish, turtles, water birds, snakes, frogs, various invertebrates, and small mammals such as raccoons, otters and even little barking dogs.

△ Sometimes a hungry gator will even resort to eating its own kind.

△ Gator jaws easily crush the shells of small turtles or horseshoe crabs.

THE "HIGH WALK"

Gators are often seen dragging themselves forward on their bellies as they slide off a bank into the water. For this reason, many people do not know that gators usually get around on land by raising their bellies off the ground and walking on their four legs. This is called the gator's "high walk." Gators can also run and have even been known to gallop for short distances. They are not adapted for running long distances but are capable of sudden bursts of speed, either to retreat into the water or to charge out of the water and onto shore to grab a morsel such as a discarded fish or perhaps a small dog. A nesting female usually charges anyone who walks too close to her nest.

Along the Anhinga Trail, Everglades National Park

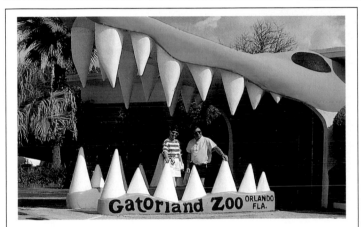

RAISING GATORS

There are a number of alligator "farms" around the state that breed gators and eventually sell the hides and meat. Several of the larger farms also function as tourist attractions. Gators are well fed with meat that has passed its safe date for human consumption, which can be purchased fairly cheaply from food wholesalers. Two of the oldest and best-known farms are Gatorland on Highway 441, just north of Kissimmee, and the St. Augustine Alligator Farm on Anastasia Island, just south of St. Augustine on Highway A1A. Don't let anyone tell you that these places raise "crocogators," the offspring of a gator and a crocodile. There are no such animals!

THE FUTURE OF GATORS

At present, the situation looks fair. Although the huge alligator populations that existed in previous centuries are a thing of the past, gators continue to be prolific breeders. Now that gator-hunting is strictly controlled, their populations are increasing wherever their habitat remains intact. The biggest current threat to the continued survival of the gator is habitat destruction such as the draining of swamps and ponds. Another threat is water pollution because it kills many of the animals that the gator needs for food. Strict laws recently enacted to protect wetlands should help prevent this kind of devastation.

WHITE ALLIGATORS: ALBINO VERSUS LEUCISTIC

Herpetologists use the word "leucistic" to describe herps that are lacking some, but not all, pigments (such as this white alligator - note the dark eyes). True albinos have no pigment in their skin and usually have pink eyes. Their eyes are pink because of the color of the blood in the partially transparent blood vessels within the eye. There is confusion about the word "albino," because it is often used loosely to describe specimens lacking some but not all pigments (as sometimes occurs in Yellow or Red Rat Snakes). Both albino and leucistic forms occur in the wild. The survival rate of these unusual and beautiful specimens is much lower than that of creatures with normal, protective coloration.

This is a Caiman, a South American member of the alligator family. It has been introduced and now breeds in South Florida.

THE LEGEND OF THE SEWER GATORS

In the past, baby gators could be bought as curios by visiting tourists. Upon returning home and eventually tiring of their new pets, as the story goes, owners would sometimes flush the little animals down the toilet, supposedly creating populations of gators in the sewers of New York and other cities. Don't believe it!

American Crocodile

Unlike the alligator, which lives in fresh water, Florida's native crocodile is an inhabitant of salt water shorelines. Never as numerous as alligators, most of Florida's 500 to 600 remaining crocodiles are found along the mangrove-bordered southern shores of Everglades National Park. There is a small colony in Estero Bay, south of Fort Myers. Another population is found on the north end of Key Largo, where artificial land-fill areas are used for nesting. Also, strange as it might seem, at least six nests and 100 hatchlings were counted in 1989 along the man-made canals that are used for cooling the water discharged from the Turkey Point nuclear power plant south of Miami. The crocodile is listed as endangered, but recent studies indicate that it is holding its own in its limited South Florida domain.

The crocodile is not as well adapted to cold weather as the alligator. South Florida is its northern limit. Nowadays, it is rare and endangered throughout its range. Colonies are found in Cuba, Jamaica, Hispaniola, coastal Venezuela, Colombia, coastal Ecuador and Peru, Central America and Mexico. Although these tropical populations belong to the same species as the Florida race, they have apparently been genetically isolated from their Florida cousins for at least 60,000 years.

Crocodylus acutus. ENDANGERED. Range in Florida: extreme South Florida around salt water. Maximum length: 15 feet.

CROCODILES VS ALLIGATORS

The crocodile can be readily distinguished from the alligator by its long, narrow snout and the protrusion of its large, fourth tooth in the forward part of its lower jaw when the mouth is closed. Although there are reports of Crocodylus acutus growing to 23 feet in South America, the record for Florida is a 15-foot male.

Crocodile

◁ *This photo shows the famous "fourth tooth" of the crocodile. Most of the crocodile's teeth are still visible when its jaw is closed. Note also the long, narrow snout.*

Alligator

◁ *The alligator lacks the protruding fourth tooth of the crocodile. Note also the shorter, thicker snout.*

A wild American Crocodile cruises through the mangroves of the Florida Keys. Notice the bright color pattern of this juvenile. This color pattern disappears as the crocodile matures.

Many people believe that crocodiles are more ferocious and dangerous to man than alligators. This might be true of the infamous Nile Crocodile and certain species from Southeast Asia, but the wild native crocodile in Florida is much shyer than the alligator, usually making a hasty retreat at the approach of a human. Whereas a female alligator guards her nest vigorously, the female Florida crocodile flees when a person approaches. Some observers say that she might go so far as to abandon her nest after humans have intruded. The scarcity, timidity, and inaccessibility of crocodiles in Florida result in little human contact. The only report of an attack on a human in Florida is a very old (and questionable) account, involving a case where the crocodile was wounded.

The female crocodile scrapes together a mound of sand and shell to serve as a nest, and lays her eggs in a cavity which she digs in the center. The mound is only about one foot high but much wider than an alligator's nest. It is always near a salt or brackish water shoreline. Some herpetologists report that the cries of the hatchlings prompt the female to open the nest and carry the babies to the water in her mouth in a series of trips. Despite such attentive maternal care, fewer than half the babies will escape hungry wading birds and other predators.

The natural diet of adult crocodiles includes water birds, small mammals like raccoons and marsh rabbits, terrapins, crabs, other marine invertebrates, and fish, especially mullet.

Unlike juveniles, the adult is slate gray with little pattern. Like crocodiles, adult alligators also lose the patterns which are prominent on the juveniles.

SNAPPING AT RAINDROPS

Despite their custom of living around salt water, crocodiles need to drink fresh water in order to avoid dehydration. One way they obtain fresh water is to sip from a thin film of rain water that floats on top of their salty bays and estuaries. They have even been observed snapping up raindrops as they fall.

◀ Mangrove-lined saltwater inlets around the edges of the Everglades National Park and the Florida Keys are the main habitat of Florida's small crocodile population. This habitat can be viewed along Card Sound Road and US 1 between Homestead and the Florida Keys. Unfortunately, many crocodiles are struck by cars while crossing these roads at night.

WAS THE BIBLICAL "BEHEMOTH" OR "LEVIATHAN" A CROCODILE?

The biblical word "Livyatan" has often been translated as "whale," but many of the passages describing this animal seem to be excellent descriptions of the crocodile.

"Under the lotus plant he lies, in the covert of the reeds and marsh…Can you…lay hands on him; think of the battle; you will not do it again!…No one is so fierce that he dares to stir him up. Who can strip off his outer garment? Who can penetrate his double coat of mail? Who can open the doors of his face? Round about his teeth is terror. His back is made of rows of shields, shut up closely as with a seal." Job 40,41. In the book of Ezekiel, the crocodile has been described as "the great dragon that lies in the midst of…rivers." Ezekiel 29:3.

The Egyptians worshipped the Nile Crocodile and built a holy city in its honor called Crocodilopolis.

Rattlesnakes

Eastern Diamondback Rattlesnake

A majestic creature, this is the most feared and dangerous snake in the United States! Its prime habitat is pine-palmetto flatwoods, although it can occur just about anywhere, even in country towns and city suburbs. It is a heavy-bodied serpent with a large triangular head and an unmistakable yellow and dark-brown diamond pattern on its back. Baby rattlers are born alive (as are those of other pit vipers) in the spring. Even the newborn can be very dangerous.

Like all pit vipers, the Diamondback uses the heat-sensitive pits just in front of its eyes to detect warm-blooded prey. A blindfolded Diamondback can still strike accurately at its target, guided by the remarkable sensitivity of its heat-detecting organs. It feeds mainly on rats, squirrels, rabbits and quail.

When threatened, the Diamondback usually coils noisily, faces its intruder, hisses, and vibrates its rattles to create a loud, high-pitched warning buzz. Although it does not jump, chase, or go out of its way to bite, it should never be teased or approached more closely than about six feet. It can strike accurately as far as half its body length, and it does not hesitate to strike anybody within its range. Most bites by Diamondbacks are the result of human carelessness.

Crotalus adamanteus. Range in Florida: entire state including most of the larger Keys. Maximum length: 8 feet.

The Big One!

RATTLERS AND BULLDOZERS

Snakes lack ears, but no one is certain that they are totally deaf. At any rate, they are very sensitive to vibrations of the ground. The movement of bulldozers at work creates strong vibrations which stir up rattlers (and other snakes) and set them in motion. Shuffling one's feet while walking in the woods may also alert a rattlesnake in the vicinity, causing it to crawl away or reveal itself by its rattle, thus avoiding a potentially nasty confrontation.

RISING FROM THE DEAD

The impulse to strike is so imbedded in the nervous system of rattlers that it may remain active for some time after the snake is apparently dead. This includes the injection of venom. Simply touching a "dead" rattler may trigger the reaction, so be very wary about approaching or handling a road kill or any other recently deceased rattlesnake.

FABULOUS FANGS

One of the most amazing specializations that occurred during the many millions of years of animal evolution was the development by certain snakes of venom glands and fangs by which they could inject their venom into other animals. These snakes were thus more assured of a kill with each strike at their prey. The fangs of rattlesnakes and other pit vipers are two elongated hollow teeth, something like curved hypodermic needles, located in the front of the upper jaw. When the jaw is

△ Some snakes (such as rattlers) have folding fangs which flip back against the roof of the mouth when not in use. This design allows the fangs to be longer and deadlier than if they were fixed in position.

closed, the fangs fold backward and are protected by a sheath of skin. As the snake opens its mouth to strike, the fangs swing out. At the moment of striking, the snake's jaws have opened very wide, and the fangs are pointing forward toward the target. The force of the snake's strike stabs the fangs into the flesh of the prey, and venom is injected. The snake's venom is produced in glands which are located below and behind its eyes. These bulging glands, on either side of the head, help give the head a triangular appearance.

When a pit viper strikes, muscles in its head squeeze venom out of the glands into small ducts that enter the base of the fangs. The venom passes through the hollow channels in the fangs and enters the body of the victim through a small hole near the tip of each fang.

Pit vipers' fangs are replaced about every three months by a pair of new fangs that grow in next to the old ones. The new fangs attach to the venom ducts before the old fangs are lost. Sometimes a rattlesnake or Water Moccasin can be found with an old fang and a new fang next to each other on the same side of the jaw. The old fangs are eventually pulled out and lost when they become embedded in the body of a prey animal. Removing a pit viper's fangs does not make it safe, since new fangs will grow to replace them.

△ The rattler strikes with its mouth open and fangs pointed mostly forward. Whether penetration is accomplished by the force of the strike or by a biting action is a question still debated by experts.

THE DIAMONDBACK'S REMARKABLE STRIKE

An Eastern Diamondback Rattlesnake strikes at prey only when it senses that it can make a kill. It strikes at a predator only when it feels extremely threatened. This contrasts with certain other snakes, such as the Western Diamondback Rattlesnake or the Water Moccasin, which often strike repeatedly with minimal provocation. The Eastern Diamondback usually needs to strike only once to achieve its objective.

How fast can a rattlesnake strike? Not as fast as lightning (the way the strike is often described), but in any case, the strike is often faster than the human eye can follow. A rattler can strike and recoil in one-quarter of a second.

Upon encountering a Diamondback, it is best to turn and walk away slowly. Running is not wise because it is always possible that there is a second rattler nearby which must be avoided also. They don't hunt in packs, but what is good habitat for one will be good habitat for others.

ALL ABOUT RATTLES

The rattle is made of a substance called "keratin," similar to human fingernails. At birth, a rattlesnake has only a single button at the end of its tail. As the snake grows, another loosely interlocking segment is added each time it sheds its skin. Many people believe that a snake's age can be determined by the number of segments on its rattle. Actually, a healthy rattler might shed its skin and add another segment to its rattles as often as four times a year. To complicate the picture, a few or even all of the segments can break off from time to time. Rattlesnakes in captivity usually grow longer rattles than wild individuals because the string of segments is less likely to be broken — up to 20 segments compared to the usual 7 to 15 for wild specimens. Long strings are sometimes faked for collectors by piecing together the rattles of several snakes.

What is the purpose of rattling? There has been much controversy among scientists over the nature and purpose of the rattle. Rattlers do not rattle when they are pursuing their prey, nor do they rattle as part of their mating ritual. The rattlesnake vibrates its tail almost always from a coiled position, the impressive stance it takes when it feels threatened. If you

have ever walked near a coiled rattler, you probably noticed that the intensity of its rattling increased as you approached closer. Like most creatures, snakes become more nervous and tense as danger nears.

Long before men appeared in the Americas, the coiling and vibrating of the rattle-tipped

tail effectively warned large animals to keep their distance. Unfortunately, the rattlesnake could not alter its ancient habit when humans invaded its domain. So, what evolved as an effective survival tactic now readily reveals the snake's presence to an enemy who can capture it or kill it from a safe distance with weapons. Instead of helping the animal survive, the rattlesnake's rattling might now be a factor leading to its extinction. Many other species of snakes, especially non-venomous snakes, rattle their tails in dry leaves to warn that they are holding their ground in self-defense.

Although totally harmless, rattles are sometimes more effective than fangs. If a grazing animal such as a cow inadvertently approaches a rattler, the snake is in danger of being trampled. A bite might not be sufficient to stop the huge, oncoming beast instantly, so the snake could still get squashed. On the other hand, a harmless warning buzz from the snake's rattle might make the cow take notice and change direction in time to save the snake. Also, it is important for a snake to save its limited venom supply for hunting, so strikes are made at non-prey animals only as a last resort when a snake feels very threatened.

RATTLESNAKE ROUNDUPS

Roundups are carnival-like events still staged in many parts of the country. For many years, San Antonio, a small town near Dade City in Pasco County, has been the site of Florida's annual rattlesnake roundup. In the 1950s and early 60s, events at the roundup included prizes for the largest, smallest and heaviest rattlers, the pitting of rattlesnakes against kingsnakes, sale of rattlesnake meat, and Gopher Tortoise races. One colorful character with a well-concealed wooden leg would show up every year and walk "dangerously" close to big rattlers. (The wooden leg, having no body heat, would not tempt the

rattlers to strike). Nowadays, the events are mostly educational and conservation-oriented.

Previously, large numbers of rattlers were captured in preparation for the roundup by flushing them out of their wintering dens in Gopher Tortoise burrows. Gasoline was poured into the burrows, and the snakes were caught as they emerged trying to escape the fumes. Since "gopher holes" are used as shelter by many creatures, this practice destroyed an important habitat in addition to upsetting the balance of nature by reducing the rattler population. This practice is now outlawed in Florida, and big rattlesnake roundups are a thing of the past. In recent years, the

San Antonio rattlesnake roundup has become primarily an arts and crafts show plus a snake handling demonstration featuring informative and environmentally sound lectures about rattlesnakes.

Not so in Texas and Oklahoma where current roundups feature such craziness as getting into zipped sleeping bags with rattlers, dodging the strikes of rattlers, skinning live rattlers, auctioning their skins, and butchering rattlers for their meat. Thousands of snakes are gassed out of their dens annually and killed, a practice which shows how little respect some people have for the marvels of nature.

▷ **Snakes are important predators, so the strong market for snakeskin products can be a factor in upsetting the balance of nature. In some poor, third-world countries where snakes are heavily hunted for their skins, agriculture has suffered losses as rodent populations exploded in the absence of natural enemies.**

△ Gopher Tortoise races with live turtles are no longer held at the San Antonio rattlesnake roundup. The enlightened organizers now entertain the kids with a new form of competition. This updated race features wooden "tortoises" that are reeled in with ropes.

SLIPPING INTO SOMETHING MORE COMFORTABLE

A healthy snake sheds its skin several times a year, a process that is called molting. The first sign of an oncoming molt is a dulling of the snake's overall color. This occurs because a new layer of skin is beginning to form beneath the old skin. Next, a lymphatic fluid spreads between the two skin layers.

A snake has no eyelids but does have scales over its eyes. When the lymphatic fluid appears between the old and new eye scales, the snake's eyes seem to be clouded over with a gray or bluish film. After about three days, the fluid is reabsorbed, and the eyes become clear again. Two to three days after the eyes clear up, the snake is ready to slough off its old skin. It begins to expand and contract its body, and the old skin soon splits around the mouth area. The snake rubs itself against branches or rough wood to help remove the old skin. The snake soon wriggles out, often leaving its former skin in one piece but turned inside out. So when you see a discarded snake skin on the ground or in the grass, its tail points in the direction that the snake crawled away.

In an ideal molt, the old skin is sloughed off in a single piece. Even the delicate eye scales are preserved. Sometimes an unhealthy or

disturbed snake does not shed its skin completely, and patches of the old skin remain attached, particularly around the head and eyes. These will usually come off with the next molt. Just after a snake sheds, its colors are brighter, and it is usually ravenously hungry.

A snake's ability to cast off its skin is considered in some cultures to be a sign that snakes know the secret of immortality. A snake displaying its bright new scales, which are prominent after shedding, seems to have been re-born.

△ **Close-up of the shed snakeskin showing that even the eyeball is covered with a single clear scale.**

DEADLY ENCOUNTERS

Although encounters with Diamondbacks are rare, it is important to be careful where you put your feet when walking through underbrush in the Florida woods, and to listen for the sound of rattles. If a person approaches a Diamondback that is in the open, it will usually coil and begin rattling when the intruder is about 15 to 20 feet away. If it is well concealed, it might not rattle at all, or it might wait until the person is dangerously close. A Diamondback can also lose some or all of its rattles, so even though it is vibrating its

tail, its warning might not be heard.

In August, 1989, a 22-year-old snake handler at Silver Springs was accidentally bitten on the back of his hand by a six-foot Diamondback. He died within two hours. The suddenness of his death was unusual, resulting from a large amount of venom injected into a major artery by a very large specimen. Antivenin is available in most Florida hospitals. If you should be accidentally bitten, force yourself to remain calm and call 911 or otherwise seek medical help immediately.

COLOR VARIATIONS

Color abnormalities are not rare in rattlesnakes. There is an area west of Gainesville where an albino rattler or a rattler with only yellow pigment is found at least once every few years.

KILLING RATTLERS

Fear and hatred of rattlesnakes is so widespread that the usual reaction of many Floridians is to attempt to kill any rattler that crosses their path. One man is known to have emptied his revolver into a rattlesnake, reloaded, and emptied his gun again. The snake kept moving and crawled away into the bushes. Incidents such as this have created the legend that a rattler will not die until the sun goes down. Actually, it is difficult to kill any snake unless the neurological tissue in its head is destroyed. The tail of a snake may be severely injured, atrophied, or dried up, and yet its front part may remain alive and functioning. This is why rolling over a rattler or any other snake with a vehicle does not necessarily kill it. Rural Floridians sometimes lock their brakes to slide over snakes they really want to kill. More enlightened thought now discourages the deliberate killing of any snakes, including the venomous species, all of which have their part in maintaining nature's balance.

NATURAL RATTLERCIDE

What animals other than man would dare kill a rattlesnake? Deer are known to stomp rattlers with their hooves. Hooved domestic animals such as sheep and horses are capable of occasional rattlercide. Alligators have been seen killing and swallowing large Eastern Diamondbacks. Bald Eagles and Red-tailed Hawks sometimes attack rattlers, although the outcome of such confrontations is not always predictable. Kingsnakes kill rattlers readily.

Rattlesnakes

Canebrake or Timber Rattlesnake

In Florida, this large and well-camouflaged snake has traditionally been called the Canebrake Rattler. It belongs to the light-colored, southern race of *Crotalus horridus*. Its favorite habitat is the slopes leading to creeks running through hardwood forests. Thus, its habitat is in the shape of a long, narrow strip. (The northern race of *Crotalus horridus* that ranges to Maine is usually called the Timber Rattlesnake. It inhabits rocky, upland terrain.)

The Canebrake is not as aggressive as the Diamondback. It usually tries to slither away when approached, but if stepped on, will probably strike. It is potentially lethal.

Crotalus horridus articaudatus. Range in Florida: the extreme north central counties. Maximum length: 6.5 feet.

Dusky Pygmy Rattlesnake

This feisty little rattler, rarely longer than 20 inches, is common throughout Florida. It lives in pine-palmetto flatwoods, scrub, and longleaf pine habitats that are not far from fresh water. It is usually gray with black blotches on its back and sides, and there is usually an orange stripe interupted by black blotches down the center of its back.

It is a hot-tempered snake, usually striking repeatedly at the slightest threat. Its venom is very potent, but the dose it delivers is small.

Sistrurus miliarius barbouri. Range in Florida: entire state, except in the Keys. Maximum length: 30 inches.

Dusky Pygmy Rattlesnake

△ Note the tiny rattles at the end of the tail. Although the Pygmy Rattler vibrates its tail when annoyed, the little rattles are barely audible, sounding more like the faint buzz of an insect. This is all the more reason to beware of this snake. Although its bite is unlikely to cause death, it can be very painful and can cause infection or tissue destruction.

Unlike most rattlesnakes, this little fellow is fond of eating frogs. Note the orange markings on the back of the head.

Cottonmouth

Florida Cottonmouth
or Water Moccasin

The Florida Cottonmouth is a serpent that strikes terror in the hearts of hikers, swimmers, and freshwater fishermen. It is a dangerous, heavy-bodied pit viper with a large triangular head.

Its coloration is variable. Older and larger individuals tend to be uniformly black, brown or reddish brown. The young are usually banded, with a dark color against a lighter background, and strongly resemble Southern Copperheads, often leading to the erroneous belief that Copperheads occur in South Florida. The Cottonmouth has a dark stripe on the cheek that runs through the eye. Its true coloration is often hidden by mud.

Most abundant in flooded woodlands, the Cottonmouth is also found around rivers, streams and ponds. It is often seen basking along the water's edge, on the bank or on a rock or log. It can also be found unexpectedly in pine woods or other dry habitats. A large part of its diet consists of frogs, but it also eats fish, small mammals and other snakes.

Unlike the harmless water snakes, the Cottonmouth tends to hold its ground rather than go immediately into the water when approached. Also, unlike other water snakes, it swims with its head well out of the water. Although it does not have rattles like a rattlesnake, it often vibrates its tail rapidly when annoyed. At the same time, it might open its mouth to reveal the whitish "cotton" lining inside. It might even expose its fangs. It strikes aggressively, and its venom is quite potent, potentially lethal.

Agkistrodon piscivorus conanti. Range in Florida: entire state. Maximum length: 6.5 feet.

The color of the adult Cottonmouth is often intense black.

◁ This Cottonmouth is older than the one shown at lower left and therefore has less yellow in its tail. Note the white of its "cotton mouth".

▽ This specimen is grayish but still has the distinctive brown stripe on its cheek, bordered by light areas above and below.

△ Note the similarity of pattern between this young Cottonmouth and the Southern Copperhead (page 20). Note also the yellow tip of the tail which is only present on very young Cottonmouths. It is used as a lure for prey. When wriggled about, it resembles a worm. This yellow tail is common to the young of many other pit vipers. It is not noticeable on rattlesnakes because the tip of the rattler's tail is covered with rattles.

CAN A WATER MOCCASIN BITE UNDERWATER?

The answer is yes, but because of water resistance, it cannot strike in its usual manner. If grabbed or stepped on in the water, the Cottonmouth would probably bite in self-defense. If it is in the water and swimmers are thrashing around noisily nearby, it will try to swim away. But moccasins are not a problem in most swimming holes because they do not like clear, open rivers and lakes.

Copperhead

Southern Copperhead

Inhabiting dry or wet areas, this handsome snake is often found around or under logs and wood piles. It is generally inoffensive, but it can be easily irritated. Herpetologists are not in agreement as to the potency of its venom. Some maintain that its bite is unlikely to result in death; others say that a well-placed bite could readily cause death. At any rate, the bite can be very painful and cause serious tissue deterioration. This snake should not be treated carelessly.

The back of the Copperhead is marked with alternating dark and light brownish bands, and the snake has two very small dark dots on the back of its copper-colored head. When coiled in a pile of leaves, it is incredibly well camouflaged — almost impossible to see. Although it lacks rattles, it often vibrates its tail when disturbed. The Copperhead is known to eat large quantities of frogs, especially in the spring. Like all Florida pit vipers, the young are born alive. Young Copperheads (and young Florida Cottonmouths) have yellowish-tipped tails which perhaps function as a worm-like lure to attract frogs.

Agkistrodon contortrix contortrix. Range in Florida: panhandle, mostly in Liberty, Gadsden, Jackson and Calhoun Counties. Maximum length: 4.5 feet.

△ Note the two small, black spots on the back of the head. In contrast to the Water Mocassin, which has different markings while immature, the Southern Copperhead keeps the same pattern throughout its life.

OWNING VENOMOUS SNAKES
Florida Statute 372.86 forbids the keeping of venomous reptiles without a license from the Florida Game and Fresh Water Fish Commission.

△ Note the excellent camouflage the color and pattern create.

△ The Copperhead's pattern is a series of hour-glass shapes.

COLLECTING SNAKES

Why do some people enjoy collecting and owning snakes? If you put this question to any snake collector, his answer will usually be that snakes are fascinating, always-interesting animals, that they are clean, and that they are not demanding as pets. Some young people get into snake-collecting because they enjoy shocking their parents or friends with their off-beat hobby. Compared to collecting something totally harmless such as stamps, snakes seem more exciting. Some people simply enjoy the flirtation with danger that snake-collecting offers. The more experienced a collector becomes, however, the less danger is involved, since he or she becomes more adept at capturing and handling the venomous species. There are, of course, some individuals who appear to deliberately handle venomous snakes in a reckless manner. Some of these unusual individuals have been bitten many times and seem to enjoy the notoriety that comes from surviving the bites of different venomous species. (It takes all kinds to make a world!) Many students, biologists and naturalists collect snakes in a spirit of genuine scientific interest. Anyone who has a sincere enthusiasm for biology, nature or the outdoors soon learns that snakes are an integral part of our environment and generally harmless, except to those people who go looking for trouble.

SNAKE TAILS

It would seem that a snake is either all tail or has no tail at all, but biologists maintain that the tail of a snake really begins at its anal opening. The length of the tail measured this way may help to identify some species.

Unlike the tails of most lizards, snake tails will not regrow if broken off. Most lizards have a weak zone in each tail vertebra which allows the tail to break off. Snakes lack these.

PIT VIPERS – IT'S THE PITS

All of Florida's pit vipers can be recognized by their stocky bodies, relatively small necks, large triangular heads, and eyes with vertical slit pupils. Of the five species of pit vipers found within the borders of Florida, only three are widespread over the state. Unlike the Coral Snake, with its "neurotoxic" venom, pit vipers produce a so-called "hemotoxic" venom that destroys the blood cells of both warm-blooded and cold-blooded animals.

There are six species of dangerous snakes in Florida. One is the Coral Snake. The other five are known as pit vipers. These are the Southern Copperhead, the Florida Cottonmouth or Water Moccasin, and three species of rattlesnakes. The name pit viper derives from the fact that there is a small depression or "pit" on each side of the face, found between the eye and nostril. The facial pits are extremely sensitive, heat-detecting organs with which the snake "homes in" on warm-blooded prey, such as small mammals and birds. The pit organs can detect differences in temperature as small as three one-thousandths of a degree centigrade.

Since there is a pit on each side of the face, they function "stereoscopically." The pits, working together with the incredible olfactory sensitivity of the snake's tongue, lead the snake unerringly to its prey, even in total darkness. The pits are sometimes mistaken for ears, but snakes have no ears.

The heat-sensing pit of a pit viper, in this case, a Copperhead

The nostril is a smaller opening used for breathing

THE HUNT FOR RED MEAT

A rattlesnake or other pit viper usually first detects distant prey by its scent. When a mammal, like a rat or a rabbit, has passed through an area, it leaves a trail of odor on the ground. Dogs can readily pursue foxes, raccoons, rabbits, and other animals by their scent trail, and believe it or not, so can a snake - by picking up the scent with its sensitive tongue. Furthermore, a pit viper's heat-detecting pits are so sensitive that they can detect faint traces of a mammal's body heat if it has passed over the ground in the previous twenty minutes or so. Following the trail as rapidly but noiselessly as possible, the snake eventually comes close enough to employ its heat-sensitive pits to zero in accurately. Some pit vipers are "sit and wait" specialists, often waiting patiently for days near animal trails or a quail feeding station for food to come to them.

If the prey is fairly large, like a rabbit or squirrel, the snake strikes, stabs with its fangs to inject venom, and withdraws instantly. It follows the weakened prey until it dies and then swallows it whole. If the prey is small, like a bird or small rat, the pit viper will not withdraw after its strike but will hold on until the animal dies in its mouth. Birds in particular are held tightly because a wounded bird can still fly some distance, leaving the snake without a trail to follow.

THE EYES TELL IT

In Florida, the eyes of all non-venomous snakes have round pupils. The venomous Eastern Coral Snake also has round pupils. The pupils of the five Florida venomous pit vipers are vertical slits. This is by no means the only way to distinguish venomous from non-venomous species, and it is not the safest way since it requires rather close inspection.

CAPTIVE BREEDING OF SNAKES

Since the mid 1970s, the breeding of captive snakes (and other herps) has accelerated as both a hobby and profession, adding a new dimension to the pleasure of collecting. Many species, subspecies and variants are being selectively bred by zoos and private individuals, and many beautiful new forms have ebeen produced. One significant result of this is that the pet trade is being supplied each year with healthy, captive-bred stock, giving wild populations some relief from the pressure of collecting.

◁ Commercial breeders Kathy and Bill Love, owners of Glades Herp, in North Ft. Myers, with four different color forms of the same species of rat snake produced by selective captive breeding.

Coral Snake

Coral Snakes have a variable amount of black pigment in their red scales. This specimen has relatively little black in its red scales and for this reason is very bright.

Eastern Coral Snake

This legendary and colorfully-banded snake can be distinguished from the Scarlet Snake and the Scarlet Kingsnake by its blunt black snout and the fact that its red and yellow bands touch each other. Like its two mimics, it is a seldom-seen burrower that is sometimes found under leaves, in trash piles, or in rotten logs. Most specimens found are less than 30 inches long. Adults feed mainly on lizards and small snakes like the ringneck.

Coral Snakes are related to sea snakes, cobras and mambas. Like their relatives, the fangs of Coral Snakes are fixed in place and inject very powerful neurotoxin. This poison attacks the nervous system, causing paralysis, suffocation or blindness. Despite the potency of its venom, the Coral Snake is a shy creature and always tries to crawl away when confronted. It does not coil like a pit viper, and it usually does not strike aggessively unless molested. There are numerous accounts of people innocently playing with Coral Snakes and not getting bitten. Despite such tales, it is foolish to take any chances with this dangerous snake!

The Coral Snake has a relatively small mouth and teeth. If it is bothered, restrained, or picked up, it usually thrashes wildly and will most likely try to bite. If it happens to find a finger, toe, or a fold of skin, it hangs on tenaciously. It might even get its teeth hooked on an arm or leg.

Two common misconceptions are that the Coral Snake's venom-injecting fangs are in the rear of its mouth, and that it must chew on its victim for some time before it can inject a dangerous dose. In truth, its pair of venom-injecting teeth are fixed in the front of its mouth, and while the Coral Snake does repeat its bite in a series of chewing movements, a large specimen can administer a dangerous dose instantly. A small Coral Snake might need to chew a while longer. In the event of a Coral Snake bite, call 911 or get the victim to a hospital immediately. Antivenin is available. Although the harmful effects of its bite usually do not occur for at least an hour or two, do not hesitate in seeking medical help.

Micrurus fulvius. Range in Florida: entire state. Maximum length: 4 feet.

△ This photo shows the belly of a Coral Snake. One of the distinguishing features of Coral Snakes is that their rings go all the way around their bodies, although the color is not as intense on their bellies. This is not true of one of the Coral Snake's mimics, the Scarlet Snake, which is white underneath. Note that this Coral Snake was prodded into raising its head. Coral Snakes, unlike rattlers and certain other snakes, do not normally rear back in this manner.

Deadly Coral Snake. It is very dangerous to pick one up. Only a professional should ever pick one up in this manner.

"RED AND YELLOW KILL A FELLOW"

This is one of the old jingles which help identify Coral Snakes. Others are: "If it has a black nose and red touches yellow, better beware, it's a dangerous fellow," and "Red on yellow, deadly fellow. Red on black, friend of Jack." "If red is next to yellow, as on a traffic light, you stop." These jingles refer to the fact that the red and yellow bands on most Coral Snakes touch each other, and this is one way to distinguish them from their mimics in the same area. Another rule is that, in Florida, if it has a black snout, it is a Coral Snake. These sayings are true regarding most Coral Snakes in the U.S. In Central and South America, however, there are many species of Coral Snakes, all marked differently. The very venomous Central American Bicolor Coral Snake, Micrurus mipartitus, has only black and orange bands. Even in Florida, some very rare specimens of the Eastern Coral Snake are all black.

CORAL SNAKE MIMICS

In Florida, the Scarlet Kingsnake and the Florida Scarlet Snake are both similar in appearance to the Eastern Coral Snake. This is not a coincidence, as these two non-poisonous snakes benefit when mistaken by a predator for the deadly coral snake. Just remember that "red touches yellow" on the coral snake (like a traffic light, so you have to stop!).

Note that in the photo at right, there are two coral snakes twined together, not one endless coral snake.

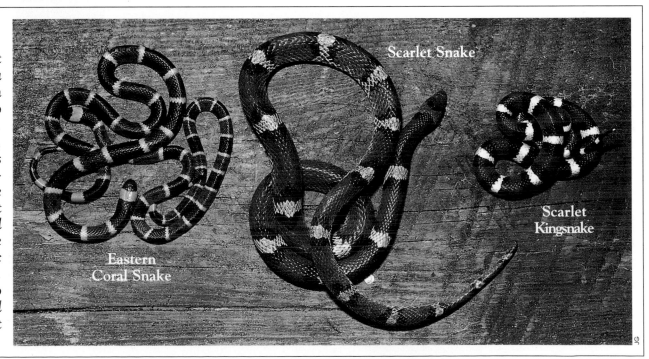

Eastern Coral Snake

Scarlet Snake

Scarlet Kingsnake

ANTIVENIN

To counteract the potentially harmful effects of a bite by a venomous snake, doctors rely mainly upon a manufactured serum known as antivenin or antitoxin. To prepare antivenin for a certain species of snake, venom from that species is first collected by forcing the snake to release its venom into a vial. Next, increasing amounts of the venom are injected into a healthy horse over a period of days. The immune system of the horse produces protective antibodies in its blood to neutralize the effects of the invading poison.

When a sufficiently high concentration of antibodies has been produced, a large amount of the horse's blood is drawn off and refined to make a serum. The serum is preserved by refrigeration. It is this serum that is injected into a human snakebite victim's bloodstream, where the horse's antibodies combine with the proteins of the snake's venom to neutralize its toxic effects.

If the victim happens to be allergic to horse blood, the effects of the serum might be very painful or dangerous. Before injecting the antivenin, a doctor will test the victim for allergic reactions. Antivenin should never be administered if the victim is allergic to it. The serum can sometimes cause more damage than the snakebite.

△ *Bill Haast and his assistant, Nancy Harold, preparing to milk a huge rattler.*

△ **Preparing to insert a rattler's fangs into the diaphragm of the venom vial.**

△ *A close-up view of the fangs shows their needle-sharp tips which are hollow for the injection of venom.*

△ *The fangs penetrate the rubber membrane, and finger pressure is applied to the venom glands.*

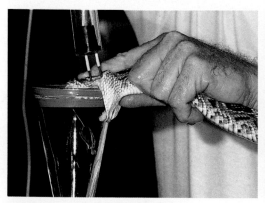

△ **Some milking operations (other than Bill Haast's) use a mild electric current to stimulate the venom glands. Note the copious flow of yellow venom.**

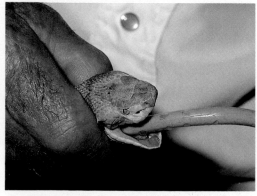

△ **When snakes are kept in captivity for milking purposes, they are force-fed a mixture of ground-up foods. The exact mix is usually a trade secret.**

POLYVALENT ANTIVENIN

Antivenin is often made by using a mixture of the venoms of various snakes from the same geographical area. In this case, the antibodies produced in the horse will counteract the venom of several species. Such "polyvalent" serum is especially valuable because most snakebite victims cannot identify the exact species of snake that bit them.

The venoms of certain species are chemically unique from all others, so that it is impossible to manufacture a polyvalent serum that covers every species. Antivenin for the Eastern Coral Snake, for example, must be made only with the venom of that species.

A VENOMOUS SNAKE BITE

This victim, a person in the business of milking snakes for their venom, was struck by a 5 1/2 foot rattler while inserting a feeding tube into its stomach. The tip of his finger was pierced by one fang. Since the snake had been milked 24 hours earlier, the dose of venom was very small, and the result should have been far less severe. But this victim had been sensitized to rattler venom by an earlier strike and suffered a life-threatening allergic reaction. He recovered after 5 days in the hospital but did not regain the full use of his finger for two months.

△ **The finger wound, immediately after the bite.**

△ **One hour later.**

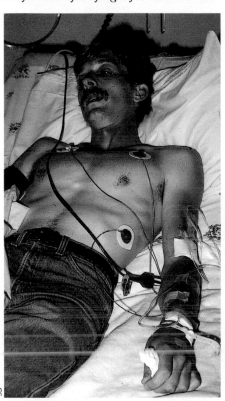

△ **Snakebite victim in hospital intensive care unit, in bad shape.**

△ **The same wound, six weeks later, showing the result of tissue destruction.**

FIRST AID FOR SNAKEBITE

Many people underestimate how dangerous and painful a poisonous snakebite can be. Although loss of life is rare, victims of snakebite often suffer for a long time and sometimes lose tissue in the area of the bite. Snake venom has evolved from digestive enzymes and, in addition to being toxic, can cause the death of tissue in the area of the bite by breaking it down in a manner similar to digestion. This may result in the need for amputation or removal of some tissue.

There are very few places in Florida more than two hours from a hospital. If bitten by a poisonous snake, concentrate on getting to a knowledgeable doctor quickly rather than attempting first aid. The venoms of Florida's poisonous snakes work slowly enough to allow an immediate trip to the hospital. If possible, call ahead to give the hospital time to locate a physician who is experienced in snakebite treatment and also time to locate and obtain the correct antivenin. First aid should be limited to applying suction. The old cut-and-suction method is no longer recommended, and neither are tight tournequets.

A "SNAKY" LIFE

Florida is home to a number of snake experts, and one of the most famous is Bill Haast (shown in photo on the previous page), who ran the Miami Serpentarium from 1947 to 1985. In addition to providing thrills for tourists, Haast has long pursued a serious scientific interest in snake venom. His pioneering techniques for collecting and marketing venom have provided a reliable source of supply for research laboratories around the world. His venom is also used to produce life-saving antivenin serums. Haast believes that snake venom (one of the most complex enzymes known to man) holds remarkable untapped potential for use in medicine. Haast, who is 82, has been bitten more than 150 times in his career and has been carried out on a stretcher 17 of those times. Haast has built up his immunity with regular injections of diluted venom (not to mention the unexpected injections he sometimes receives). But even for him, the bite of a deadly snake is a painful and dangerous matter, an ongoing hazard of his chosen career. After describing the terrible effects of a recent cobra bite, Haast was asked if that was the last time he had been bitten by a snake. Haast replied, "That was the last time I was bitten by a <u>cobra</u>!"

SNAKE PEOPLE—BORN IN THE YEAR OF THE SNAKE

Unlike the twelve-month cycle of western astrology, Chinese astrology is based primarily upon a cycle of twelve years. Each year is named for one of the twelve animals which came to bid Buddha farewell when he left the earth. A person's character follows the nature of the animal which rules the year of his birth. That animal is said to be "hiding in his heart." Persons born in the year of the snake* are shrewd in business, possessive, demanding and tenacious. Snake people love the good life. Snake men are often handsome and powerful, while snake women are high-strung, physically attractive and ambitious. Most snake women dress elegantly, yet tastefully.

The ability of a snake to shed its skin symbolizes the snake person's ability to emerge from conflict unhurt. Snake people born in winter are more docile as this is the time of hibernation, while those born in summer are more dangerous characters. The snake person is sometimes ruthless but always independent and determined, and is considered likely to achieve fame and fortune. Chinese astrology recognizes monthly (lunar) cycles as well as annual (sun) cycles. The sign of the snake is loosely related to Taurus.

*1905, 1917, 1929, 1941, 1953, 1965, 1977, 1989 (Chinese years begin in February by the western calendar, so persons born in January, 1990, are also snakes).

▷ Postage stamp from the People's Republic of China representing the Year of the Snake, 1989. This stamp has been enlarged to show the rich details of the artwork.

中国人民邮政 8分

己巳年

T. 133.(1-1) 1989

Earth Snake

Smooth Earth Snake

This little snake and its close cousin, the Rough Earth Snake, *Virginia striatula*, are only occasionally found in peninsular Florida. The Smooth Earth Snake is light brown with flecks of darker brown. It has smooth scales. The Rough Earth Snake is dark brown with a light yellow or cream underbelly. Its scales are keeled but glossy. Look for these snakes in pinewoods, under boards and debris, and in damp, sandy terrain. They apparently feed on insects, earthworms, and small snails.

Virginia valeriae valeriae. Range in Florida: mostly north Florida and the panhandle. Maximum length: 13 inches.

Red-bellied Snake

Florida Red-bellied Snake

This very secretive little snake is found in damp wooded areas. It burrows in moist leaf litter and decaying wood and feeds on earthworms and other small invertebrates. It can be plain brown, black or gray, with a red, orange or yellow belly. Four faint dark stripes run along the back, and three yellowish spots on the neck fuse to form a "collar." It is common in some northern states (Pennsylvania and Michigan) but rare in Florida.

The Latin name, *occipitomaculata*, means "eye spot" and refers to the little white spot below the eye.

Storeria occipitomaculata obscura. Range in Florida: northern peninsular Florida and eastern panhandle. Maximum length: 15 inches.

FLORIDA'S NON-VENOMOUS SNAKES

Florida has more species of non-poisonous snakes than any other state east of Texas, a total of 37 different species. There are only 6 species of poisonous snakes in Florida, so the poisonous snakes are relatively rare. Three species of non-poisonous snakes found in Florida are found nowhere else in the world: the Short-tailed Snake, Florida Crowned Snake, and the Rim Rock Crowned Snake.

Florida's non-poisonous snakes come in a great variety of sizes and colors and are found in all Florida habitats from mangrove swamps to the driest scrub, from limestone spring runs to the Everglades, and even the backyard. However, many of Florida's non-poisonous snakes are becoming far less common, and some are now protected by law, so be sure to check the latest wildlife regulations before keeping a snake as a pet.

OPHIDIOPHOBIA (FEAR OF SNAKES)

The great majority of snakes are not venomous, but the occasional bite from a venomous serpent gets widespread publicity, generating unwarranted fears of snakes in general. In the last 25 years, deaths resulting from snakebite in Florida have averaged fewer than one per year! Statistically, death by snakebite is far less likely than being killed by lightning.

Along with spiders, snakes suffer more human misunderstanding than any other animals. Some say their bad reputation began in the Garden of Eden. After the biblical serpent successfully tempted Eve to eat the fruit of the Tree of Life, "The Lord God said to the serpent, 'Because you have done this, cursed are you above all cattle and above all wild animals; upon your belly you shall go, and dust you shall eat all the days of your life.'" Genesis 3:14-15. In addition to receiving the blame for this incident, snakes are feared in part because of the very few species which are actually dangerous and in part because of ignorance about their mysterious ways. In fact, most snakes are beneficial and are truly fascinating once fully understood. Snakes have been so maligned and mistreated that their populations have been severely diminished in many parts of the world, and Florida is no exception.

Recently, keeping snakes as pets has mushroomed as a hobby. This trend might help bring about a better understanding of snakes among the general public, although intensified collecting will put pressure on wild populations. Children certainly do not have an ingrained fear of snakes. Fear is usually passed on to them by their parents or other adults.

Brown Snake

Florida Brown Snake

This small brownish snake usually inhabits the edges of freshwater ponds, ditches, and cypress heads, often near human habitation. It can be distinguished by two rows of dark spots running down the length of its back. Also, it usually has a light-colored band just behind its small head.

Although it may strike when cornered, its mouth is not large enough to inflict a bite. It feeds on slugs, snails and earthworms.

This species is related to garter snakes and water snakes and, like them, bears live young rather than laying eggs.

Storeria dekayi victa. THREATENED IN THE LOWER KEYS. Range in Florida: peninsular Florida and the lower keys. Maximum length: 15 inches.

IT'S ALL IN THE WIGGLE (HOW SNAKES MOVE)

The motion of snakes has always been a mystery. Even the Bible describes "the way of the serpent upon a rock" as something too wonderful to understand (Proverbs 30: 18-19). Part of the confusion comes from the fact that snakes have different ways of propelling themselves.

The best-known method is called "serpentine motion" or "lateral undulation" and is the familiar S-curve crawl. By applying pressure against irregularities on the ground from various points along its long body, a snake almost magically converts side-to-side motion to forward movement. A trail left in the sand by this kind of movement will appear as a narrow, winding path. However, on a smooth surface where a snake cannot get good traction, it will writhe vigorously with little forward movement. The trail left along such a surface would be a wide track as the snake's whole body slides forward. All snakes can swim and they make use of the S-curve movement to propel themselves through the water.

A snake can also move by first anchoring its front belly scales into the ground or other surface (by applying pressure), bunching up its loose skin so that the skin slides forward along the body, anchoring its rear scales, and then sliding its body forward within the skin. Such forward motion leaves a trail that is more like a straight line. This kind of movement (called rectilinear) is slower, but it is useful for stalking prey and climbing up the rough bark of a tree. *The scales of a snake's belly overlap, with the sharp edges pointing toward the rear. This helps the snake get traction against the ground for forward movement.*

Another kind of movement consists of a back-to-front rippling motion (vertical, caterpillar-like ripples) which also leaves a straight trail. A fourth kind of motion, completely different from the others, is used by the desert sidewinders. The snake's overall movement is lateral and leaves a series of "J" marks in the sand. Sidewinders are not found in Florida, but Hognose Snakes use a sidewinding-like locomotion on loose sand.

I'll come back to you, Sidney!.. But I won't crawl!

© Gary Larson/Chronicle Features

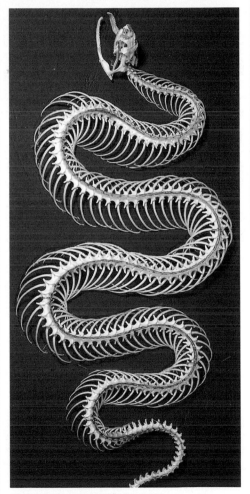

SNAKE SKELETONS

The snake skeleton consists of hundreds of vertebrae joined together by special connectors in addition to the normal ball and socket joints which provide great flexibility. When a snake eats a large meal, the thin skin between its hard scales stretches to allow great expansion of its body. A snake's skeleton can accomodate this expansion because snakes do not have the restrictive bones of humans such as the breast bone or the pelvic girdle.

Water Snakes

(Reddish phase)

Florida Water Snake

This common and often beautiful aquatic serpent is sometimes seen on roadways during rainy weather. Quite variable in color, it may be reddish, black-and-white banded, or mostly black. It is also called the Florida Banded Water Snake. It feeds mainly upon fish and frogs. When disturbed, it flattens its body, and the head assumes a triangular shape similar to that of a venomous pit viper. Though harmless, this species usually tries to bite upon being captured. Some individuals are surprisingly docile, but it is sensible not to try grabbing a large one with bare hands. Like most water snakes, the young are born alive.

Nerodia fasciata pictiventris. Range in Florida: peninsular Florida around fresh water. Maximum length: 5 feet.

Florida Water Snake (black phase)

△ The Florida Water Snake's Latin name is *pictiventris*, or "painted belly." This specimen displays iridescence over a brown and white pattern. Other specimens may have a dark and light pattern composed of red and yellow plus several other colors.

COTTONMOUTH LOOK-A-LIKES

Almost all species of Florida's large, non-venomous water snakes are, at times, mistaken for the venomous Cottonmouth, which often leads to their being killed wantonly. Most water snakes feed mainly on fish. They are sometimes attracted in large numbers to the shallow, freshwater ponds in which fish are bred at commercial fish farms, where they are likely to be captured or killed by the dozens. In the wild, water snakes are generally very wary, and swim away quickly if anyone approaches. When captured, larger ones almost always try to bite. They also release a moist, creamy, foul-smelling substance called "musk" from glands near the anus. At the same time, they might defecate, which helps spread the musk on the captor's hands and arms. Handling these often-beautiful snakes is usually not a pleasant experience, although they can become fairly docile in captivity.

Florida Green Water Snake

Despite its name, this common water snake is not always conspicuously green. It is more often dark olive to brown. It is heavy-bodied when full grown and may be mistaken for a Water Moccasin. It likes to bask in vegetation over water and can be seen in weedy marshes and grasses around ponds and along canals. It feeds mainly on minnows and small fish. This snake often bites aggressively when first handled, and it also emits a nasty-smelling musk. However, it usually becomes docile in captivity.

Nerodia floridana. Range in Florida: entire state except western tip of panhandle. Maximum length: 6 feet.

SNAKES IN POOLS

At Florida homes which are built near swampy areas, it is not unusual to find a snake (or a turtle or alligator) in the swimming pool. Many snakes need to get into water every few days to moisten their skin and control parasites. But they would not remain for long in a swimming pool. Unlike a mouse which would probably be trapped in a pool and doomed to die, a snake can easily climb out.

◁ **A roaming water snake being removed from a swimming pool.**

Brown Water Snake

Found around creeks, canals, rivers and ponds, this handsome water snake is often mistaken for the Florida Cottonmouth. It can be distinguished by the dark brown blotches along its back and sides which contrast with a lighter brown background. It feeds mainly on fish, which it pursues from along the shoreline. It can sometimes be seen hanging in vegetation above water. It has a reputation for biting aggressively, so it is wise not to try picking up a large individual with your bare hands.

Nerodia taxispilota. Range in Florida: entire state. Maximum length: 6 feet.

SLIMY SNAKES?

People are often heard referring to snakes as "slimy" creatures. Quite the contrary, snakes are definitely not slimy, even those that might seem to be. Their bodies are covered with a tough skin composed of neatly joined scales that shed water better than a duck's back. In fact, their scales are generally so dry and clean that they can pick up human fingerprints.

Water Snakes

Redbelly Water Snake

This beautiful water serpent is sometimes called the Copperbelly. As an adult, its back and sides are a rich reddish or chocolate brown, and its belly is bright orange. It has keeled scales and appears to have a very rough skin. The young have dark blotches on their backs with dark crossbars on the sides. This snake is most at home in river swamps and is usually a very shy creature, fleeing into the water at the slightest disturbance. One of its most interesting behaviors is hanging from vegetation just over water with its mouth open to the flow, grabbing fish that happen to swim by. It also feeds on frogs. Like most water snakes, it tries to bite upon first being handled and releases a terrible-smelling musk.

Nerodia erythrogaster erythrogaster. Range in Florida: northwestern peninsular Florida and the panhandle. Maximum length: 5 feet.

Glossy Crayfish Snake

This rarely seen snake derives its scientific name, *rigida*, from the fact that its body is comparatively stiff. One of its nicknames is Stiff Snake. Its usual habitats are cypress ponds and sloughs in flatwoods. Its top is shiny brown, and a thin dark stripe runs down each side. Its belly is yellowish and has two rows of spots that are shaped something like half-moons. It feeds on crayfish, small fish, frogs and dragonfly nymphs.

Regina rigida rigida. Range in Florida: north Florida and the panhandle. Maximum length: 30 inches.

Striped Crayfish Snake

The diet of this interesting aquatic snake consists solely of crayfish and dragonfly nymphs. It lives around ponds and sluggish waterways and seeks refuge among water hyacinths and other aquatic vegetation. It is an iridescent brown on top with three darker stripes down the back. Its belly is a smudged yellow. Like many other aquatic snakes, it can sometimes be seen crossing roads on rainy nights.

Regina alleni. Range in Florida: peninsular Florida and eastern panhandle. Maximum length: 2 feet.

Florida Water Snake
encircling minnows
in a shallow pool

Brown Water Snake
eating catfish

HOW WATER SNAKES FEED

Water Snakes use at least three different methods to find their prey. They may sit still and wait for fish and frogs to pass close enough for a quick strike. Or, they may forage along the bottom, checking in holes and under rocks for prey. Some snakes swim through shallow water with their mouths open. When using this method in shallow tidal pools, the snake may form a loop with its body and then close the loop smaller and smaller, running its open mouth along its own body hoping to catch any fish within the loop. The saltmarsh snakes use this technique to catch fish trapped in small pools at low tide.

Black Swamp Snake

This small, glossy, black snake with a red belly is found in freshwater ponds and ditches, usually among entangled roots of water hyacinths and other aquatic vegetation. It feeds on frogs, tadpoles and small invertebrates. Sometimes it is seen at night after a heavy rain. It is timid and does not bite.

Seminatrix pygaea. Range in Florida: all of Florida except the extreme western panhandle. Maximum length: 18 inches.

It is also
called the
Red-bellied
Swamp Snake

THE SPEED OF SNAKES

While some snakes appear to move very quickly for a short distance over the ground or through vegetation, their over-all speed is not fast, and even the fastest snake cannot outrun a human. In terms of "running" speed, the coachwhips and racers are the fastest Florida snakes.

Some snakes can strike at blindingly fast speeds, although the distance a snake can strike is only about half its body length. (But keep in mind that the average snake is strong enough to turn and bite the hand that is holding it up by its tail.) In terms of striking speed, rattlesnakes have no equals, although rat snakes and kingsnakes also move faster than the eye can follow when striking.

Water Snakes

Mangrove Water Snake

This snake, though not rare, is infrequently seen because of its preference for dense mangrove swamps. Its color is variable and can be orange, straw-colored, or gray. It has rough scales. It feeds on small fish and other small aquatic creatures that get trapped in shallow water when the tide goes out. Living in tidal areas, it is served potential meals twice a day.

Nerodia clarki compressicauda. Range in Florida: coastal south Florida, up the west coast to Tampa. Maximum length: 3 feet.

Red phase

Dark phase

◁ The Mangrove Water Snake is highly variable in color as these photos show. The lighter, redder phases are less common.

Gulf Salt Marsh Snake

This is the only black-and-yellow-striped snake that lives in Florida's brackish or salt water habitats. There are four stripes down each side of the body, two light and two dark.

This snake prowls mainly at night. Its diet includes fish and various marine invertebrates such as small crabs. Like most water snakes, it tries to bite when first captured but calms down in captivity.

Nerodia clarki clarki. Range in Florida: along the coast from Levy County to the tip of the panhandle. Maximum length: 3 feet.

Atlantic Salt Marsh Snake

This small water snake is only found in the saltmarshes along Florida's East Coast. Since most of this coastline has been developed, much of its habitat has been diked and drained, and there is continuing pressure from further development.

This snake is easily recognized by its three light stripes on a dark background. The stripes are most distinct behind the head and are more broken toward the tail.

This species lives in tidal marshes where it hides in crab burrows by day and emerges at night to feed on very small fish. It captures these fish when they become trapped in isolated pools of water left on bay bottoms at low tide (see box titled "How Water Snakes Feed," page 31).

Nerodia clarki taeniata. THREATENED. Range in Florida: East Coast of Florida between Daytona Beach and Ft. Pierce. Maximum length: approximately 2 feet.

Ribbon Snakes

Southern or Peninsula Ribbon Snake

This common, slender relative of the garter snakes is often seen crossing roads or basking in vegetation near water. It feeds voraciously on insects, frogs, small fish, salamanders and other pond life.

When startled, it simply glides away smoothly through the vegetation rather than dropping abruptly into the water in the manner of a water snake.

Its color is variable but usually brownish, with a tan stripe down its back and each side.

This snake will sometimes try to bite when handled and will release musk.

Thamnophis sauritus sackeni. THREATENED IN THE LOWER KEYS. *Range in Florida: all of Florida east of the Apalachicola River. Maximum length: 40 inches.*

▲ This photo shows the head of a typical non-poisonous snake (a Peninsula Ribbon Snake). Compare this head to the head of a pit viper. The opening in the snout here is not a heat-sensing pit but a nostril. Snakes use their nostrils for breathing only. They smell with their tongues (see page 43).

Bluestripe Ribbon Snake

This attractive subspecies of ribbon snake is usually distinguished by the prominent blue stripe along its sides. The Bluestripe Ribbon Snake is found in the Gulf Hammock region, an area along the Gulf of Mexico from Tallahassee to Crystal River. Hammocks are plant communities composed of broad-leafed or hardwood forests (not pines, like much of Florida). The Gulf Hammock is a wet hammock, traversed by lots of rivers and streams. It is one of the wildest parts of Florida. This is the same habitat as that of the Bluestripe Garter Snake, a snake with the same color pattern. It is interesting and puzzling that these two blue snakes share the same range.

Thamnophis sauritus nitae. Range in Florida: big bend area of northwest Florida from Pasco to Wakulla County. Maximum length: 40 inches.

Garter Snakes

Bluestripe Garter Snake

Similar in habits to the Eastern Garter Snake, this beautiful subspecies is distinguished by the prominent pale blue stripe along each side.

Thamnophis sirtalis similis. Range in Florida: big bend area of Gulf coast from Pinellas County northward into the panhandle. Maximum length: 4 feet.

Bluestripe Garter Snake

Eastern Garter Snake

Eastern Garter Snake

This often beautiful snake gets its name from its resemblance to the garters worn by women of earlier generations. Its colors can be quite variable, but in Florida it is generally a distinctive turquoise or blue-green, with light stripes and black spots arranged in rows. Its scales are strongly keeled, which gives its skin a rough look and feel. It is almost always found near water where it feeds on toads, frogs, fish and other small aquatic animals. Like all garter snakes, it bears its young alive. When captured, it often releases musk and usually tries to bite.

Thamnophis sirtalis sirtalis. Range in Florida: entire state. Maximum length: 4 feet.

Mud Snake

Eastern Mud Snake

This interesting, highly aquatic snake is shiny black above and red-and-black-blotched underneath. It lives in and around fresh water, where it feeds in the mud on sirens, amphiumas and other aquatic creatures. The female pictured here laid 60 eggs.

The Eastern Mud Snake has a pointed tail with which it usually tries to poke a human captor, but this weapon cannot break the skin. This is a snake that will not bite.

Farancia abacura abacura. Range in Florida: entire state except western tip of the panhandle. Maximum length: 6.5 feet.

▽ Most of what is seen in this photo is the underbelly of the Eastern Mud Snake.

THE TERRIBLE ROLLING HOOPS

Both the Mud Snake and the Rainbow Snake are sometimes called Hoop Snakes because, according to folk tales, they hold their tails in their mouths and roll like a hoop after their human victims! Next, they supposedly use their sharp-pointed tails to stab their victims to death. Needless to say, this is a myth. Both snakes are completely harmless and, although large, do not even try to bite upon being handled. Though both have a pointed tail, it will not penetrate human skin.

Rainbow Snake

This colorful water serpent is one of Florida's most beautiful snakes, but it is rare and difficult to find. It has red, black and yellow stripes, and immediately after shedding it has an almost iridescent appearance.

The Rainbow Snake is usually found among floating vegetation in freshwater streams and sometimes in loose sand along the banks of waterways and swamps where it feeds mainly on eels. In Florida it is most often found in spring runs and the rivers they feed. Naturally, this snake is difficult to keep in captivity because of its specialized feeding habits. This is a nocturnal species and is rarely seen in broad daylight.

Farancia erytrogramma erytrogramma. Range in Florida: north Florida including the panhandle, south to Marion and Lake Counties and the St. John's River Basin. Maximum length: 5.5 feet.

SNAKE SCALES AND OTHER SMALL THINGS

"Every thing made by human hands looks terrible under magnification—crude, rough and unsymmetrical. But in nature every bit of life is lovely. And the more magnification we use, the more details are brought out, perfectly formed, like endless sets of boxes within boxes."

Roman Vishniac, in Andreas Feininger, <u>Forms of Nature and Life</u>, Viking Press, Inc. NY 1966. (Roman Vishniac was one of the pioneers in microphotography.)

SNAKE SCALES

Snakes have either "smooth" scales or "rough" scales. The smooth-scaled snakes are the sleekest and shiniest. If you examine their scales closely, you can see that they are flat, smooth and glossy. Rough scales are also called "keeled" scales. In the center of each is a slightly raised ridge or keel. When every scale on a snake's skin has a little keel, the overall appearance and feel of such a snake is slightly rough rather than sleek.

There is no known difference in function between the rough and smooth scales. In fact, the Rough Green Snake has a close relative living in the northern part of the United States, the Smooth Green Snake. They both make their living the same way.

Snake scales are not separate plates but are actually just hardened folds in a one-piece skin.

Smooth scales of the Indigo Snake

Rough scales of the Redbelly Water Snake

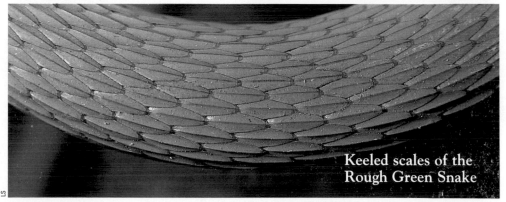

Keeled scales of the Rough Green Snake

Pine Woods Snake

This small, orange-brown snake is fairly rare but may be seen in and around moist pine flatwoods, particularly after heavy rains. Its belly is yellowish, and its lips and chin are light-colored. It has a thin, dark line that runs from the nose through the eye to the corner of its mouth. Although it has a mild venom, it makes no attempt to bite and may be considered harmless to humans. It feeds on small lizards and frogs. The Pine Woods Snake belongs to a large group of tropical snakes (more than 50 species in Central and South America), but is its only representative in North America. Since Florida extends down into tropical regions, it marks the northern-most range of a number of tropical species (the Indigo Snake is another example).

Rhadinaea flavilata. Range in Florida: most of Florida from the Lake Okeechobee area northward. Maximum length: 16 inches.

▷ This photo reveals why the Pine Woods snake is sometimes called the Yellow-lipped Snake.

NON-VENOMOUS SNAKE BITES

Many people get bitten by non-venomous snakes, particularly when trying to pick them up in the wild. Almost all large water snakes bite readily, as well as racers, coachwhips, garter snakes, pine snakes and rat snakes. All of these except coachwhips become more docile in captivity and cease to bite. The teeth of these species are small but cause lacerations. To avoid infection, it is a good idea to squeeze as much blood out of the wound as you can, and then douse it with alcohol or another antiseptic.

Florida Pine Snake

This attractive snake inhabits pine woods and pine scrub, a drier habitat than that of the Pine Woods Snake, a creature with whom it has almost nothing in common other than a similar-sounding name. Its base color is whitish or gray, and on its back it has variable-colored blotches. It hisses loudly and often tries to bite upon first being picked up. As the pocket gopher is its preferred prey, it is most easily found in dry, sandy areas where active pocket gopher burrows are abundant. Pine snakes spend most of their time underground.

Pine snake populations are dwindling. Captive breeding has been successful, but this snake is seldom bred in Florida because even captive-bred offspring cannot be sold or traded.

Pituophis melanoleucus mugitus. SPECIES OF SPECIAL CONCERN. Range in Florida: entire Florida mainland in dry, upland habitats. Maximum length: 7 feet.

◁ Note the large rostral (nose) scale used for digging. This burrowing snake spends a lot of time underground, often in the burrows dug by pocket gophers, where it searches for gophers to eat.

Immature

HOW SNAKES SWALLOW LARGE PREY

A snake has four rows of teeth in its upper jaw. The outer two rows can move independently of each other and the middle rows in a back and forth, rachet-like motion. This helps the snake work large prey slowly but surely down its throat. The inner two rows of teeth are less moveable.

The lower jaw consists of two sides which are connected at the front not by bone but by elastic tissue. This allows for back-and-forth motion of the lower teeth and also allows the snake to spread its lower jaw wider to accommodate large-sized meals.

A snake's teeth are not used for chewing, only for swallowing. The snake's many small teeth all point backwards. Once a snake has grabbed a prey animal in its mouth, any further movement of its jaws forces the prey farther and farther down its throat.

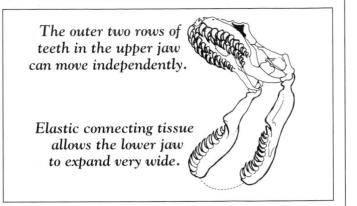

The outer two rows of teeth in the upper jaw can move independently.

Elastic connecting tissue allows the lower jaw to expand very wide.

EASTERN GARTER SNAKE VS. SOUTHERN TOAD

At first glance, it appears that it would be impossible for this snake to swallow such bulky prey. However, with their uniquely constructed jaws, snakes are well equipped to perform such feats.

△ The snake's jaws can open very wide because of a special hinge arrangement. To protect themselves, some toads swell up with air to make themselves too big to swallow. Some snakes (like the hognose, but not this garter snake) have long teeth which they use to puncture and deflate a puffed-up toad for easy swallowing.

△ The snake's jaws work first on one side and then the other as its backward-pointed teeth slowly draw the toad into the mouth. Contrary to the sequence shown here, snakes usually eat their prey head-first. The legs (and hair, if it is a rodent) fold more readily in a backward direction so swallowing is easier. Prey eaten feet first takes much longer to swallow.

△ Goodbye, Mr. Toad. Snakes occasionally die from trying to swallow prey that is too large. After a snake swallows its prey, it usually has a large bulge in its middle for a couple of days.

△ Burp! A meal this size will take days to digest. This snake will digest the entire toad, bones and all. A pet snake should not be disturbed while it is digesting a meal.

Ringneck Snake

Southern Ringneck Snake

This is a very common but reclusive little snake that is usually about 8 to 12 inches long. It is frequently found around homes, where it is often seen by people who are gardening or pulling up grass. Its back and sides are black or dark gray. It has a yellowish ring around its neck, with a small break at the top, just behind the head. Its belly is a very rich yellow, becoming deep orange near the tail, with a row of black triangular spots. When disturbed, the Southern Ringneck often coils its tail to show the bright underside. It is harmless and makes no attempt to bite. Its diet includes earthworms, slugs, amphibians, small lizards and newborn snakes.

Diadophis punctatus punctatus. Range in Florida: entire state. Maximum length: 18 inches.

◁ The defensive display of the Southern Ringneck presents the bright underside of its tail to frighten away a predator or draw the predator away from the Ringneck's head.

▽ Note the distinctive pattern of half-moons along the belly of the Southern Ringneck. Northern and Western Ringnecks have different patterns on their bellies.

△ This photo reveals the small size of the ringneck in Florida. In the western states, ringnecks grow much larger.

Key Ringneck Snake

This little snake really should have a different common name. Although it is a subspecies of the Southern Ringneck Snake, it does not have a neck ring or has only a faint vestige of one. At present, its existence is threatened due to commercial development, but the preservation of lands for the endangered Key Deer may also offer a refuge for this little gray-headed snake, as well as for the many other species and subspecies that are found nowhere in the world but the Florida Keys.

Diadophis punctatus acricus. THREATENED. Range in Florida: Big Pine Key and the Torch Keys. Maximum length: 18 inches.

◁ The Key Ringneck Snake has only a faint ring around its neck. Compare this to the more obvious and distinct ring of the Southern Ringneck Snake.

Racers

Southern Black Racer

This slender, graceful, and fast-moving snake is often found near human settlements and in cities. It is probably the most frequently seen snake in Florida, particularly by city dwellers. This is because it is large and is active during the daytime. It breeds and thrives in urban and suburban residential areas where there are likely to be mice and rats. Although it spends most of its time on the ground, it is an accomplished climber and is frequently seen in shrubbery around homes. It is not poisonous but can be counted on to bite upon capture. It is easy to recognize by its jet-blackness and its prominent white chin. Its eyes are reddish. It preys not only upon rats and mice but also upon frogs, toads, lizards, birds, and other snakes. Despite its species name, *constrictor*, it does not kill its prey by constriction; it swallows its prey alive.

Coluber constrictor priapus. Range in Florida: most of the Florida mainland and the Lower Keys. Maximum length: 6 feet.

Baby Black Racer

Note the white chin

△ "*Eeek*, a snake in the garden" usually means that a Southern Black Racer has been spotted. This is the snake most likely to be seen in backyards because it is big, it moves about in the daytime, and it lives in residential neighborhoods. It is an important part of nature's pest control system and should not be disturbed.

◁◁ The pattern of the hatchling Black Racer shown in the photo at far left is very different from the adult. Every time it sheds, it becomes blacker and turns totally black when it reaches about 2½ feet in length.

Everglades Racer

This is a subspecies of the Southern Black Racer that does not have the latter's jet black coloration. It is either grayish or blue-green above, and its underside is whitish with a tinge of blue.

Coluber constrictor paludicola. Range in Florida: Everglades, Big Cypress Swamp and the Upper Keys. Maximum length: 6 feet.

Brown-chinned Racer

The habits of this subspecies are like those of the Southern Black Racer. It is distinguished from the latter by its slaty black color and its tan or brown lip scales and throat.

Coluber constrictor helvigularis. Range in Florida: Florida panhandle in the Apalachicola and Chipola River valleys. Maximum length: 5 feet.

Green Snake

Rough Green Snake

This is Florida's only slender, bright-green snake. It has rough or "keeled" scales which distinguish it from the Smooth Green Snake found in the northern U.S. Rough Green Snakes are very well camouflaged when climbing in vegetation but are not usually difficult to capture once they have been spotted. Their teeth are very small and they will not try to bite.

In the wild they feed on crickets, grasshoppers, spiders and other small invertebrates. They do poorly in captivity and should not be held in confinement for more than a few days.

Opheodrys aestivus. Range in Florida: entire state. Maximum length: 3.5 feet.

▷ Green snakes are great climbers. It is rare to see them on the ground.

Coachwhip

Eastern Coachwhip

This large and graceful serpent is found mostly in dry habitats. It is the fastest-moving snake in the state when it decides to make a hasty retreat. It preys primarily upon lizards, mice and small birds. When molested or handled, it tries to bite incessantly.

The authors once witnessed a young coachwhip surrounded by a flock of screaming Scrub Jays. Suddenly the snake lashed out and grabbed a bird by its leg. The panicked jay flew about two hundred feet and disappeared into the woods with the coachwhip still hanging on.

If captured and placed in a terrarium, coachwhips usually strike at the glass every time someone comes near, eventually damaging their noses badly. They should not be kept in tight confinement.

△ This long, slender snake gets its name from the pattern of its scales which gives it the look of a braided leather whip. Some specimens are black at the front and tan over the rest of the body. Other specimens are nearly all tan. Note the striking appearance of its eye.

Masticophis flagellum flagellum. Range in Florida: entire state. Maximum length: 8.5 feet.

Indigo Snake

Eastern Indigo Snake

The beautiful and graceful Indigo is Florida's largest native snake. It derives its name from the dark blue iridescence of its large scales. The blue color is most noticeable just after the snake has shed. It feeds on toads, frogs, rodents and other snakes, including venomous ones. It grabs its prey in its powerful jaws and swallows it alive. The Indigo was originally found throughout the state, but it is now becoming scarce in some areas due to overcollecting and habitat destruction. It shares Gopher Tortoise burrows with rattlesnakes and other animals. It is illegal to capture or own this snake without a permit, and it cannot be sold commercially.

Drymarchon corais couperi. THREATENED. Range in Florida: entire Florida mainland, Key Largo and the Lower Keys. Maximum length: 8.5 feet.

△ The Indigo Snake uses its heavy body to hold its prey but does not kill by strangling like snakes which are constrictors.

△ Although the Eastern Indigo is the largest American snake (with many specimens over 6 feet and the record over 8 feet), it is short indeed when compared to the world record Anaconda of South America, which has been measured at 37 feet in length.

The Indigo Snake is sometimes called the Blue Gopher because it is so often found in burrows of the Gopher Tortoise.

△ Many specimens of Indigo Snakes have reddish chins and throats. Compared to the Southern Black Racer (page 39), the Indigo has a much thicker, heavier body.

THE SHOWBIZ INDIGO

The Indigo Snake tames easily. Since it is very big and impressive, it was formerly used in carnival side shows. Because of the obvious male sexual symbolism of snakes, female side-show entertainers sometimes employed this large snake in their acts in a very suggestive and vulgar manner.

Hognose Snakes

Eastern Hognose Snake

Dry, sandy habitats are home to this remarkable reptilian actor (see box). It feeds almost exclusively on toads, using its turned-up (hog-like) nose like a shovel to burrow after them under the surface of the ground. The Eastern Hognose is quite variable in color. It may be entirely black above or have patterns that combine black with yellow or white. It may also show red, orange or khaki green.

Heterodon platyrhinos. Range in Florida: entire state. Maximum length: 3.5 feet.

△ The coloration of the Eastern Hognose varies from jet-black to golden yellow (see photo on page 43). In Florida, the gray phase is the most common.

◁ In the defensive display of the hognose, the ribs are spread to the sides, flaring the skin. This is often accompanied by a simulated strike in which the hognose thrusts forward but does not even open its mouth.

Southern Hognose Snake

The Southern Hognose is found in dry habitats. It is a secretive burrower and feeds mostly on small toads. It is cream or beige with dark blotches along its back and sides. Often there is a tinge of orange present between the blotches. Most specimens of this little snake are shorter than 20 inches. This species is much less commonly encountered than the Eastern Hognose.

Heterodon simus. Range in Florida: all of the state north of Lake Okeechobee. Maximum length: 2 feet.

△ Unlike the Eastern Hognose, the Southern Hognose has only one color phase.

▷ The shovel-shaped rostral scale of the hognose's snout is used to dig up Spadefoot Toads.

FAKING IT

Both species of hognose snakes in Florida go through unbelievable antics if threatened. When first approached or disturbed in the wild, a hognose inflates its neck like a cobra and hisses. It might also try a coiling routine in an attempt to mimic a rattlesnake.

If this initial play-acting does not frighten away its molestor, it might next roll over on its back and play dead, even opening its mouth and letting its tongue hang out. It goes so far as to wallow, get sand in its open mouth, and vomit.

If the "dead" hognose is picked up at this point, it is completely limp. It would seem that it is really dead. But if left alone, it soon recovers its composure and slinks off. (You can even imagine it chuckling to itself.) Despite such exaggerated histrionics, it is a harmless snake and a good candidate for Florida's most entertaining reptile.

△ Snakes have no eyelids, so even when playing dead, a snake cannot close its eyes.

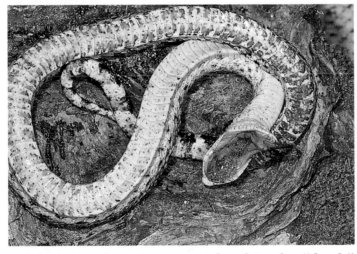

△ Maximum theatrics are employed in the "death" scene.

△ Even when picked up, a hognose playing dead will remain limp.

THE CLOUDY EYE

A cloudy eye is the first sign of that a snake will soon shed its skin. Snakes getting ready to shed are less active. People who keep snakes seldom try to feed them at this time because they usually won't eat until they have completed shedding.

THE OPEN DOOR

Snakes don't have to open their mouths when flicking out their tongues because they have a notch in the rostral scale of the upper lip which provides enough opening for the tongue to come out anytime. The snake shown in this photo is an Eastern Hognose.

SMELLING WITH A FORKED TONGUE

The forked tongue of the snake has inspired many legends and myths. Among the common fallacies is the belief that a snake's tongue is the source of its venom, or that it can sting by sticking out its tongue. Venom is actually delivered through the fangs, not the tongue.

Furthermore, the tongue has no taste buds. So what is the true purpose of the snake's very busy tongue? Like the membranes in our noses, the snake's flicking tongue captures scent particles from the air and the ground. When the tongue is pulled back into the mouth, it transfers these particles to the lining of two cavities, called Jacobson's organ, on the roof of the snake's mouth. This sensitive organ is connected to the brain by olfactory nerves. Although snakes also smell through their nostrils in the usual manner, their tongue-flicking is a much more efficient and sensitive means of smelling. When a snake is exposed to a new odor, such as the scent of a nearby mouse, it intensifies its tongue-flicking rather than breathing more rapidly.

Rat Snakes

Red Rat Snake or Corn Snake

This always-attractive snake can vary considerably in its color patterns. One color phase lacks red altogether. This is one of the most conspicuous and popular snakes in the state and is often seen in residential areas. It may be the least feared of all of Florida's larger snakes, because many people recognize it right away, and most know that it is an efficient rat catcher. It is often bred in captivity, and many different color forms are propogated, including albinos. Adults feed almost exclusively on mice and rats, which they kill by constriction before swallowing them head-first.

Elaphe guttata guttata. SPECIES OF SPECIAL CONCERN IN THE LOWER KEYS. Range in Florida: entire state. Maximum length: 6 feet (average length: 3 to 4 feet).

CATCHING SNAKES

When herpetologists need snake specimens, one time-honored method of securing them is to go out at night (or send some graduate students) to cruise rural roads, especially during light rain. Snakes crossing roads at night tend to linger to absorb the heat of the day retained in the pavement. Capture of non-venomous snakes consists of jumping out and grabbing them (the hunter, of course, must know how to handle snakes.)

TWO KINDS OF RAT SNAKES

Florida has only two species of rat snakes, Elaphe guttata, the Red Rat Snake, and Elaphe obsoleta, which appears in three different geographic color variations: the Yellow, Gray, and Everglades Rat Snake. None of the latter interbreed with the Red Rat in the wild, but they readily interbreed with each other wherever their ranges overlap, resulting in many more color variations.

Rat snakes are among the most valuable Florida snakes because of their skill in killing rats and mice. They are easy to tame and are popular as pets.

IT'S JUST A PHASE – THE COLOR OF SNAKES (RED RAT SNAKES AS AN EXAMPLE)

Naturalists, including herpetologists, often refer to a certain color or pattern of an animal as a "phase"— like the "gray phase of the Screech Owl," or the "Miami phase of the Red Rat Snake." When used in this way, "phase" does not mean a temporary condition; it means a distinct color variant of a species. When the reference is to a geographical area, it means the color variant of the species that is usually found in that area. Albino variations are also a kind of color phase.

Almost all species of snakes show individual and geographic variation. Some species are highly variable, especially rat snakes, king snakes, water snakes, and hognose snakes. Often a certain color phase may be common within a limited area and rare elsewhere. For example, a rare yellow phase of the Eastern Diamondback has been found several times in the small area between Gainesville and Trenton, Florida, a distance of about twenty miles.

An individual snake can undergo remarkable color changes during its growth from newborn to adult. For instance, Black Racers are gray with reddish-brown blotches when born, but they turn jet-black as they grow old. Snakes do not go through annual cycles of color change (like some birds), but their colors are always brighter just after they shed.

△ This Red Rat Snake is close to a true albino, but there is still a remnant of the yellow color.

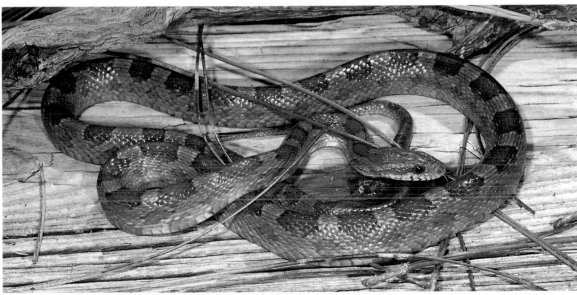

◁ This Red Rat Snake is partially albinistic. It lacks black pigment.

△ The Red Rat Snake in the Florida Keys was once considered a subspecies called the Rosy Rat Snake. Although it is no longer classified as a true subspecies, the name is sometimes still used for Red Rat Snakes found in the Keys. This variant is a bit smaller, averaging 2 to 3 feet. Its color is straw-yellow or light orange but seldom rosy or pinkish, despite its name.

△ This rat snake was created by captive breeding and lacks black and yellow pigment, hence its blood-red color.

▷ The gray phase of the Red Rat Snake occurs mostly between Lake Okeechobee and Ft. Myers.

Rat Snakes

Yellow Rat Snake

This snake is a powerful constrictor and is the best tree climber of all Florida snakes. It can often be seen sticking its head out of holes in trees. As its name implies, the Yellow Rat Snake feeds mainly on rats, but it also feeds on birds, squirrels, and other small mammals. The familiar yellowish subspecies *quadrivittata* is the most common variety and is usually a dull yellow with four broad dark stripes running the length of its body.

When handled, the Yellow Rat often releases a moist, creamy musk from glands near the anus. The musk has a distinctive, pungent odor. Interestingly, both wild and domestic cats respond to the smell as they do to catnip! A Wild Kingdom documentary once showed a Florida bobcat wallowing and frisking in the musk of a Yellow Rat Snake.

Elaphe obsoleta quadrivittata. Range in Florida: most of peninsular Florida and the Keys. Maximum length: 7 feet.

△ The bright yellow form of the Yellow Rat Snake shown above is found in the northern and central parts of Florida. Note the black tongue.

◁ The most common form has darker markings and dull yellow as shown in this photo.

▷ The juvenile Yellow Rat has blotches rather than stripes.

Gray Rat Snake or Oak Snake

This attractive snake is found mostly in wooded areas around swamps. It is almost always light gray with dark markings. It is usually quite docile except when first caught. Since it is often sold in pet stores, it is a familiar Florida snake even outside its natural range in the panhandle. Interestingly, the hatchlings and juveniles of all the Florida forms of *Elaphe obsoleta* look like adult Gray Rat Snakes. The yellow and orange forms develop their adult colors after the first year.

Elaphe obsoleta spiloides. Range in Florida: Florida panhandle and east to Baker and Bradford Counties. Maximum length: 7 feet.

ALL THE SNAKES IN IRELAND

Did St. Patrick really chase all the snakes out of Ireland in the fifth century? According to some scientists, there never were any snakes in Ireland. This would not be as surprising as it seems. Ireland is a cold place and could have been iced over in ancient times. Cold-blooded creatures need the warmth of the sun to survive. There are many places in the world that have no snakes including some warm, but isolated, islands, such as Hawaii and a number of other South Pacific islands.

Gulf Hammock Rat Snake

Formerly considered a distinct subspecies, this variant is now recognized as an intergrade between the Gray Rat Snake of the panhandle and the more typical *quadrivittata* form of Yellow Rat Snake. Each individual seems to be marked differently, but most have blotches like the Gray Rat Snake and stripes like the Yellow Rat Snake.

Elaphe obsoleta williamsi. Range in Florida: Gulf coast from Pinellas County northward to Dixie County. Maximum length: 7 feet.

△ Gulf Hammock Rat Snake eating a Barking Tree Frog. Snakes use this head-first method far more often than the feet-first method illustrated on page 35.

△ Each Gulf Hammock Rat Snake seems to be marked differently, but most have blotches like the Gray Rat Snake and stripes like the Yellow Rat Snake.

Everglades Rat Snake

This is an orange subspecies of *Elaphe obsoleta* which sometimes totally lacks the customary dark stripes. Although it has a limited range, it is common in some areas. Its tongue is totally or partially red, unlike the black tongues of other rat snakes. The brightly colored specimen on the front cover is less common than the duller one shown below.

Elaphe obsoleta rossalleni. Range in Florida: Everglades and Big Cypress Swamp. Maximum length: 7 feet.

THE KEYS RAT SNAKE

At one time the rat snake found in extreme southeastern Florida and the upper keys had its own name: Elaphe obsoleta dekerti. This rat snake is more greenish. It is no longer recognized as a subspecies distinct from the Everglades Rat Snake.

PUTTING THE SQUEEZE ON—HOW CONSTRICTORS KILL

Rat snakes are constrictors. A rat snake locates its rodent prey through its sense of smell. Stalking close to the prey, it suddenly strikes and grabs with its jaws. Faster than human eyes can follow, the snake wraps several coils of its long body around the chest and stomach area of the rodent, maintaining enough pressure to prevent it from breathing. Within a minute or two, the rodent dies of suffocation. The snake then searches for the head and proceeds to swallow its prey whole. Rat snakes are great climbers and will ascend into tree tops to get at birds' and squirrels' nests.

Other constrictors native to Florida include kingsnakes and the Florida Pine Snake.

The largest snakes in the world are constrictors. These are the Reticulated Python from Southeast Asia and the Anaconda from South America. Full-grown specimens of these snakes can subdue and eat prey the size of a deer. After all, both grow to lengths of about 30 feet!

Short-tailed Snake

This seldom-seen, pencil-thin snake lives in sandy soils of upland areas. It is found nowhere in the world but Florida. It is usually gray, with dark blotches along its back and sides, but there are several different color forms. Sometimes it also has orange spots on its back. When handled, it hisses and tries to bite but is not dangerous. Collecting it is now illegal. Little is known of its habits, but it seems to eat nothing except the black-headed crowned snakes of the genus *Tantilla*.

Stilosoma extenuatum. THREATENED. Range in Florida: central Florida and Gulf coast counties from Pinellas north to Columbia and Suwannee Counties. Maximum length: 25 inches.

Scarlet Snake

This beautiful little banded snake is reputedly a mimic of the venomous Eastern Coral Snake. It has a red snout instead of the shiny black nose of the latter. Also, its banding does not follow the color pattern of the Eastern Coral Snake, and the bands do not circle the whole body but stop on its sides; its belly is plain white or yellowish.

The Scarlet Snake likes to burrow and can sometimes be found under trash piles or logs. Sometimes it can be seen crawling around at night after a heavy rain.

The Scarlet Snake is very docile and makes no attempt to bite when handled. It has a reputation for being difficult to keep in captivity, but if you put about three inches of sandy soil mixed with some sphagnum moss in a terrarium, it seems to feel quite at home. Place a flat piece of wood in the terrarium under which it can hide. Some captives will eat raw, beaten eggs served in a shallow plate. In the wild its main food is reptile eggs. If it begins to lose weight, this obviously means that it is not eating and should be released.

Cemophora coccinea. Range in Florida: entire state. Maximum length: 32 inches.

◁ The white belly of the Scarlet Snake distinguishes it from the Eastern Coral Snake. Note also that the tip of its snout is red whereas that of the Eastern Coral Snake is black.

▷ This Scarlet Snake is ready to shed. Its pattern is obscured by the separation between the old skin and the new skin.

DO WE REALLY WANT ONE OF THESE UNDER EVERY HOUSE? EXOTICS ON THE LOOSE IN FLORIDA

For years, tales have been told about huge or venomous exotic snakes on the loose in Florida. In one story, a load of Egyptian Cobras escaped in the early 1970s from a wrecked truck south of Clewiston. The snakes supposedly became established in the sugar cane fields, thriving on rats and occasionally terrifying a field hand. (This story got into National Wildlife Magazine.) Another story tells of an Anaconda that was released years ago in the Big Cypress Swamp, not far from Monroe Station. The snake supposedly grew to monstrous size and was reportedly seen from time to time. From the dubious to the real: On the night of June 28, 1989, David Spaulding of Fort Lauderdale heard a loud squealing in his backyard. Walking outside to investigate, he was staggered with disbelief and perhaps a little fright when he saw a 20-foot, 250-pound Reticulated Python (shown above) wrapped around a raccoon. A few days later, he discovered that the huge Asian serpent was living under his house, apparently having resided there for years.

The owner of Pesky Critters Relocation in Miami finally succeeded in moving the snake to a new home. It was concluded that the python had been released perhaps 15 years earlier in Hugh Taylor Birch State Park which borders Spaulding's property. The animal had survived well by eating raccoons and other wildlife in the park, and occasionally a pet from the neighborhood, "gobbling them up like marshmallows," according to Spaulding.

Although this story has a happy ending, it might have been otherwise. A snake this size could easily kill a child. The story serves as a strong warning against the release of exotic animals in any strange environment, a practice that has often led to disastrous consequences in Florida and elsewhere.

Crowned Snakes

Coastal Dunes Crowned Snake

Crowned Snakes are the smallest native snakes in Florida, with an average adult length of about 10 inches. There are five recognized species and/or subspecies in the state. They are similar in appearance: tan or light brown to reddish brown with black heads. The most common crowned snake in Florida is the Peninsula Crowned Snake.

Crowned snakes are venomous but are not large enough to be harmful to humans. They are called "rear fanged" because their small venom fangs are in the rear of the upper jaw. Crowned snakes feed mostly on beetle larvae but may also eat small centipedes and spiders.

One subspecies, the Rim Rock Crowned Snake, is one of the rarest snakes in Florida and perhaps in the entire United States. It

Coastal Dunes Crowned Snake

inhabits some of the remaining tropical hardwood hammocks around limestone outcroppings.

The various crowned snakes in Florida are distinguished primarily by small differences in the markings on their heads. The Coastal Dunes Crowned Snake has a bit of white on its black head and nose.

Tantilla relicta pamlica. Range in Florida: coastal dunes from Cape Canaveral to Palm Beach County. Maximum length: 8.5 inches.

AT LEAST THIS EXOTIC WON'T STRANGLE ANY DOGS

The Brahminy Blind Snake, Ramphotyphlops bramina, is the only exotic snake known to be breeding in Florida. It was intoduced from Asia and is common around Miami where it is established in sod nurseries. It is now spreading around the state. One interesting feature of this snake which helps it prosper is that it does not need a mate to reproduce. It is self-fertilizing (parthenogenic). It is indeed blind, and its front end looks very much like its tail end. It lives mostly underground and eats termites and ant larvae.

49

Kingsnakes

Scarlet Kingsnake

Compared to other species of kingsnakes, the Scarlet Kingsnake is quite small. It is a burrower and seldom seen. When handled, it tries vigorously to escape and will sometimes bite, although its small mouth and teeth do little harm. It is sometimes found under the bark of rotting pine stumps, under rotten logs and trash piles, or on roads at night. It feeds mainly on small skinks, anoles and baby mice.

Lampropeltis triangulum elapsoides. Range in Florida: entire Florida mainland and possibly Key West. Maximum length: 30 inches.

△ The color between the black bands of the scarlet Kingsnake can vary from white to yellow or orange.

△ The bands continue around the belly (like the Eastern Coral Snake).

DON'T CONFUSE A SCARLET KINGSNAKE WITH A CORAL SNAKE
This is another beautiful mimic of the Coral Snake. It, too, has a red snout like the Florida Scarlet Snake. Its bands completely circle the body like those of a Coral Snake, but the pattern of banding is different. Its yellow bands are bordered on each side with black bands so that, unlike the Coral Snake, the yellow does not touch the red.

Mole Kingsnake

This medium-size kingsnake is a secretive burrower, very rare in the areas of Florida where it is known to occur. It seems to prefer prairies which periodically flood (such as the Kissimmee Prairie). Not much is known about its habits in Florida except that in captivity it eats small mammals and lizards. There are several color variants which have well-separated dark blotches on the back and sides, with a lighter background.

Lampropeltis calligaster rhombomaculata. Range in Florida: panhandle, with several isolated colonies in the peninsula down to Lake Okeechobee. Maximum length: 3 feet.

Florida Kingsnake

The Florida King is the most numerous of the Common Kingsnake subspecies and is found from Gainesville to well south of Lake Okeechobee. Although highly variable, this is the best known kingsnake that is truly Floridian. Its scales are usually yellowish at the base and are tipped with mahogany or chocolate brown. In the southern part of the Everglades it is replaced by the Brooks Kingsnake. Although populations are declining in many areas of the state, this species thrives in certain man-modified environments, such as the ditches and canals bordering the sugar-cane fields south of Lake Okeechobee.

Lampropeltis getulus floridana. Range in Florida: Gainesville to south of Lake Okeechobee. Maximum length: 7 feet.

▲ Florida Kingsnake, another form.

▲ Baby Florida Kingsnake.

FOUR KINDS OF COMMON KINGSNAKES

There is only one species of Common Kingsnake in Florida (Lampropeltis getulus), but it occurs in various color forms. There is some confusion as to how the forms should be classified. Are they color variants, geographical variants, or separate subspecies? Currently, herpetolgists recognize four subspecies of Common Kingsnakes in Florida (Florida, Chain, Blotched, and Brooks). However, these subspecies interbreed in the areas where their ranges overlap, creating other variants. Starting from the northern part of the state and going south, the number of bands of the Common Kingsnake increases as does the light pigment between the bands.

Although Common Kingsnakes are large and powerful serpents, they are harmless to humans. Besides eating other snakes, they also feed on birds, mice, turtle eggs, rats and other small mammals. Kingsnakes are becoming rare in many parts of Florida where they were once common. This may be related to the loss of wetlands where these snakes are most abundant.

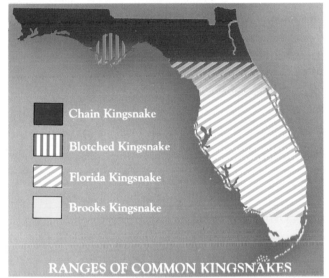

■	Chain Kingsnake
▥	Blotched Kingsnake
▨	Florida Kingsnake
□	Brooks Kingsnake

RANGES OF COMMON KINGSNAKES

▲ **Notice that the ranges of the common kingsnakes overlap in several areas.**

Chain or Eastern Kingsnake

The subspecies of Common Kingsnake most often found in North Florida is the Chain Kingsnake, which is found north of Gainesville. The name Chain Kingsnake comes from the light-colored markings over a dark, usually black, background.

Lampropeltis getulus getulus. Range in Florida: North Florida. Maximum length: 7 feet.

THE KINGSNAKE DIET

Although kingsnakes are best known for eating other snakes, another important item in their diet, in Florida, is turtle eggs. If a kingsnake locates a fresh turtle nest, it can excavate it with its snout and fill up on eggs.

Kingsnakes

Brooks or South Florida Kingsnake

The Brooks Kingsnake or South Florida Kingsnake is found only in the Everglades and usually south of the Alligator Alley toll road (now I-75). This beautiful subspecies has a more speckled appearance overall than Florida's other basic kingsnake forms, generally with a lavish sprinkling of yellow, and more crossbands.

The Brooks Kingsnake is so popular in the pet trade that populations in some areas have been affected by over-collecting.

Lampropeltis getulus brooksi. Range: southern Everglades. Maximum length: 7 feet.

THE ADVANTAGES OF HATCHING FROM EGGS

The female snakes which lay eggs do not remain gravid (carrying eggs) for as long a period as those that bear their young alive. This is an advantage some snakes share with birds.

Snakes usually lay their eggs in cavities in trees, rotten logs, abandoned railroad ties, under rocks, or in depressions in the ground. They don't make nests and don't guard or tend to the eggs (with the exception of the King Cobra of Southeast Asia).

Snake eggs are leathery and therefore less brittle than the eggs of birds. They are therefore somewhat less vulnerable and don't require as much care. The snake hatching from the leathery shell shown at right is a Florida Kingsnake.

KING OF THE SNAKES

Kingsnakes derive their name from their habit of killing and eating other snakes, including rattlesnakes, to whose venom they are immune. The kingsnake first bites another snake in the head or neck and then kills it by constriction, later swallowing it head-first—a long meal, so to speak.

Kingsnakes are so aggressive that even with their own kind, the bigger snake will sometimes kill the smaller. Just a few days after hatching, baby kingsnakes start trying to consume each other. For this reason, captive kingsnakes must be kept in separate terrariums.

Blotched Kingsnake

The Blotched Kingsnake is a rare form of the Common Kingsnake found only in a small area of the panhandle near the Apalachicola and Ochlockonee Rivers. As its name suggests, it often has dark blotches. The blotches appear over a background of cream-colored spots on each scale. Sometimes the blotches are absent, and it may have dark stripes or be completely speckled instead.

Lampropeltis getulus goini. Range in Florida: panhandle around the Apalachicola and Ochlockonee Rivers. Maximum length: 7 feet.

▽▷ These photos show three color forms that are all variations of the Blotched Kingsnake. At right, a variety with stripes instead of blotches. At lower right is a form with the blotches totally absent. Below is a specimen on which the dark blotches are prominent, but note that they are widely spaced.

WHAT IT MEANS TO BE COLD-BLOODED

Reptiles and amphibians are called cold-blooded because they do not have an internal mechanism that allows them to maintain a constant body temperature (like birds and mammals). Instead, they take on the temperature of their surroundings. This means that in cold weather they feel cold to the touch. Scientists call such animals "ectotherms," referring to their use of external heat. Their primary souce of heat is direct sunlight, which explains why so many reptiles (and some amphibians)· like to bask. They also absorb heat from warm surfaces and this explains why snakes are often found on black-topped roads at night (the asphalt retains the heat of the day). Some cold-blooded animals attempt to regulate their body temperature by moving back and forth from direct sunlight to shade or cool burrows.

Being cold-blooded has both advantages and disadvantages. The body temperature of any animal must reach a certain level before it can be active. Cold-blooded creatures must rely on their environment for this heat. On cold or cloudy days and during winter, they may not be able to be active or may be so sluggish as to become easy prey for predators. This is not a problem for warm-blooded animals (endotherms). They turn food into heat through a chemical reaction in the cells of their bodies. However, this heat production requires high metabolism and can be a very expensive proposition. Birds and mammals must eat and burn a lot more food than cold-blooded animals of the same size. For example, there are cases of snakes surviving on only one or two meals a year.

This helps explain why reptiles and amphibians can do so well in harsh environments such as deserts. For example, there are several kinds of toads and turtles living in desert environments which pop out of the ground during annual rains. They feed, reproduce, and then return to the ground when the temporary pools dry up. They can live underground for the rest of the year on food they stored away in a few weeks time. Warm-blooded animals cannot do this, but, on the other hand, warm-blooded animals can survive in cold regions where no reptiles or amphibians can be found.

"Well, of COURSE I did it in cold blood, you idiot! I'm a reptile!"

SNAKE SEX

Male snakes can usually be distinguished from females of the same species by their longer tails. That is, the distance from the anus to the tip of the tail is relatively longer in males. The male's tail is also thicker because it contains two penises, sometimes called hemipenes. They are kept tucked inside except when in use.

During the mating season, males can locate females by smelling their pheromones (scents that are sexually attractive). Upon encountering a receptive female, the male initiates a courtship ritual which usually involves rubbing his chin along her body and the top of her head. Eventually, the two snakes line up their bodies with their cloacas (common opening for reproduction and excretion) pressed together. The male hemipenes are stored inside-out within the tail. At copulation, one of the two hemipenes (depending upon which side the male approaches from) is turned right-side out as it is everted into the cloaca of the female.

The length of time that the male and female stay joined together varies among species. It is rarely less than ten minutes, but with some species, such as the Eastern Diamondback Rattlesnake, the union can last as long as 24 hours .

△ This is the hemipenes (or dual penis) of a preserved specimen of a hognose snake. Each penis has a bifurcated (double) head, so this snake (and a number of others) really has a double-double penis. Although all snakes have twin penises, not all species have penises with double heads.

The penises of live snakes are rarely seen because they are only extended during copulation and are extended directly into the female while the male and female are pressed tightly together. No one knows why a snake needs to have two separate penises. Only one at a time is used for copulation. Naturally, there has been speculation about one male mating simultaneously with two females, but the only known report has remained unconfirmed and is generally regarded as a hoax.

SNAKES AS HYPNOTISTS

Many people believe that snakes have the ability to hypnotize their prey. This idea often appears in stories and cartoons (such as Walt Disney's "Jungle Book"). Although not true, it is easy to see how this idea originated. A snake's eye has a "glassy stare" because it has no moveable eyelids, so a snake cannot blink or close its eyes. Many of the animals upon which a snake preys defend themselves by freezing in the face of danger. Indeed, many snakes have trouble seeing creatures which are not in motion. So it would not be unusual to find a snake staring face to face with a motionless animal and to imagine that the snake has somehow mesmerized its victim.

Great Blue Heron eating a water snake

WHAT CREATURES PREY ON SNAKES

Birds, cats, alligators and other snakes are Florida's most important predators of snakes. Alligators will not hesitate to kill and eat large Diamondback Rattlers as well as other species. Small birds and house cats often subdue baby snakes. Bobcats, panthers, hawks, herons, and egrets are very active predators of non-venomous snakes. Birds kill a snake by biting or crushing its head with their beaks, swallowing the snake head-first. Kingsnakes, Indigo Snakes, and Coral Snakes are hunters of other snakes. Kingsnakes kill snake prey by constriction, Indigos overpower their victims, and Coral Snakes paralyse their prey with a powerful neurotoxin venom.

SECRETS OF THE SNAKE CHARMER

In some parts of the world, particularly in India, street performers seemingly charm venomous cobras into rising out of a basket and swaying to the sound of a flute. Since snakes have no ears and most likely cannot hear even one note of music, these mesmerized performing serpents are really swaying in response to the movements of the charmer and his instrument. The mouths of these venomous snakes are sometimes sewn shut or the fangs removed. Actually, herpetologists are uncertain of how much or how little snakes can hear. However, it is known that snakes are quite sensitive to vibrations.

SNAKES IN MYTH AND RELIGION

△ In Penang, Malaysia, there is a Buddhist temple known as the Snake Temple because of the poisonous serpents which prowl freely around its altars. The snakes appeared mysteriously when the temple was constructed and made the place their home. The faithful worshippers decided that the snakes were a good omen and would serve as protectors of their temple. Through the years the snakes have indeed added to the temple's income by making it a popular tourist attraction.

△ In Thai legend, a cobra saw the Lord Buddha sitting in a muddy area meditating. The serpent crawled under the Buddha and used its coils to support his body. It then spread the hood of its head to shade the Buddha from the sun.

△ In Singapore, large pythons are kept at various Taoist temples. One of the Chinese Gods is depicted with one foot resting upon a serpent and the other upon a turtle. The pythons are handled, sometimes by small children, during religious ceremonies, thus creating interest. Among the faithful, these big snakes are considered intermediaries to the gods.

In mythology, the caducius was a winged staff given by Apollo to Hermes, the messenger of the gods. It supposedly had the power to end conflict. To test it, Hermes put it between two battling snakes. The snakes immediately gave up their struggle and wound themselves peacefully around the staff. In ancient times the caduceus was used as a symbol of peace. In modern times it became the symbol of the medical profession, **Caduceus** perhaps because of its resemblance to the staff of Ascepius, the Greek healer, which had a single serpent entwined, but no wings. In mythology, snakes symbolize life and health (perhaps because they shed their skins and appear fresh and reborn). Even in the Christian Bible the snake is not always the symbol of corruption depicted in Genesis. In Numbers 21:6-9 the snake is a symbol of healing. Amazingly, a snake entwined around a staff symbolized the healing arts in the ancient cultures of many widely separated civilizations including that of India, the Aztecs, and the North American Indians. The Greeks apparently inherited it from the Mesopotamians who had used this symbol for thousands of years. **Staff of Ascepius**

The use of snakes in religious ceremonies is not limited to exotic cultures in countries half a world away. The Hopi Indians of the American Southwest use snakes in religious ceremonies. They place snakes in the crevices of rocks to take messages to the underworld. There are still religious snake cults in parts of Appalachia. Members pass around rattlesnakes and copperheads in the belief that their faith will protect them from venomous bites. The dangerous snakes do not always respond as expected. The unfortunate results of these activities spawned several well-publicized lawsuits against church leaders for damages suffered.

Spadefoot Toad

Eastern Spadefoot Toad

This fascinating creature gets its name from a specialized "spade" on the heel of each hind foot that is used for digging backwards into the soil, as deep as eight inches. Although quite common, Spadefoot Toads are rarely seen because they spend most of their time underground during the day, emerging only on warm, humid nights to feed. A combination of very heavy rainfall and low barometric pressure lures them by the thousands to perform their intense mating ritual. This might occur only one or two nights per year. Hordes of them seem to appear suddenly out of nowhere, hopping across country roads and suburban streets just after dark, as they head for flooded fields, saturated lawns and drainage ditches.

When a suitable stand of water is found, the males begin calling from the surface. To call, the male simultaneously inflates his large throat pouch, closes his eyes, and lets go with a loud, mournful-sounding *yaaouwk* (see page 62). The call is repeated every five to ten seconds. When a female has been attracted by the call and swims nearby, the amorous male grabs her quickly. Sometimes, a desperate male might grab onto a pair of Spadefoot Toads that are already mating, creating a rather frenzied "ménage à trois."

Scaphiopus holbrookii. Range in Florida: entire state including Key West. Maximum length: 3.25 inches.

◁ Spadefoot Toads can be distinguished by their yellowish eyes and vertical pupils. They sometimes have a wild-eyed look but are in fact quite harmless. Their skin secretions might be irritating, so it is advisable to wash well after handling one.

In Florida, Spadefoot males tend to be yellowish and females brownish. Compare the mating pair shown on page 62.

◁ The arrow shows the "spade" of the Spadefoot Toad which is actually a scale-like appendage that helps the toad in digging. The entire foot is rather thick and hard, and the whole foot is used like a living shovel.

Spadefoots can indeed dig fast and bury themselves very quickly. The hardened skin which forms the "spade" of the Spadefoot Toad is possessed by all members of this group. They all spend much of their lives buried in the ground.

Southern Toad

This is the most familiar Florida toad and is found in all habitats. It is the one most likely to be seen hopping around homes (or convenience stores) at night, looking for a meal under insect-attracting lights. It is also the toad usually seen on roads on rainy nights when it is foraging for food or crossing to ponds for breeding.

In the daytime or in dry weather, the Southern Toad usually burrows into the ground.

Generally it is grayish, but dark-brown or reddish specimens can be found. It has two prominent ridges between the eyes ending in conspicuous knobs behind the eyes. These are called "cranial knobs." On rainy nights, its call is a continuous high-pitched trill that can be deafening up close or in chorus.

Bufo terrestris Range in Florida: entire state. Maximum length: 4.5 inches.

REPTILE OR AMPHIBIAN?

Since both reptiles and amphibians have backbones, they are both vertebrates. Both are cold-blooded, which means that their body temperatures and their levels of activity are determined by environmental factors such as air temperature, sunlight and water temperature. In general, they rev up their metabolism and are more active when the weather is warm.

Amphibians include frogs, toads, and salamanders. Amphibians usually lay their eggs in water, and when the larvae hatch they resemble little fish (the tadpole stage), taking oxygen from the water by means of gills. Later, their bodies undergo a change called metamorphosis. During this change most species acquire lungs and legs. Most amphibians then leave the water and venture out onto land, breathing air through their nostrils. They tend to live around bodies of water or in damp places. Those that have adapted to living in dry areas burrow down into the ground to avoid drying out. The skin of most amphibians remains soft and moist throughout their lives.

Reptiles include alligators, crocodiles, turtles, lizards and snakes. Although some reptiles spend their lives in and around water, their eggs are not laid in water but on land. When the young hatch from the eggs (or are born alive, as with some snakes and lizards), they are instantly air breathers. The young look like miniatures of the adults. The skin of reptiles is dry and is made up of tough plates called scales.

Fowler's Toad

Fowler's Toad is usually brown or gray and can be distinguished by the dark spots on its back, each spot containing several warts. It lacks the pronounced cranial knobs of the Southern Toad. It has a line running down its back like an Oak Toad, but the line is not as prominent. It is an attractive animal and is very common throughout its range in the eastern United States. Very small Southern Toads are difficult to distinguish from Fowler's Toads.

Bufo woodhousii fowleri. Range in Florida: western panhandle. Maximum length: 3.75 inches.

WHAT GOOD ARE TOADS?

If considered only for their economic value, they rate as very beneficial to humans because they eat large numbers of insects.

Oak Toad

This is the smallest species of toad in the United States. Found in pinewoods and oak hammocks, it can also be seen in towns and cities, particularly in wooded suburbs. While it might be mistaken for a young Southern Toad, the Oak Toad is darker, much smaller, and lacks cranial knobs (see previous page for details about cranial knobs.) Most significantly, it has a conspicuous light-colored line running lengthwise down the middle of its back. Its call sounds like the peeping of a chick, but much louder. While calling, the male's throat pouch extends upward in front of his face like a small inflated sausage.

Bufo quercicus. Range in Florida: entire Florida mainland and the Lower Keys. Maximum length: 1.25 inches.

TOADS, FROGS AND WARTS

Handling a toad or frog does not cause warts! However, a few Florida toads and frogs produce toxic or foul-smelling substances in their skin, and it is wise to wash well after handling them. By all means, do not transfer their skin secretions to the eyes or mouth.

In the rainforests of Central and South America, there are many brightly-colored frogs whose skin secretions can be lethal if accidentally introduced into the bloodstream. In fact, there is one species of the so-called "arrow-poison frog" in the jungles of northwest Colombia whose skin toxins are so powerful that merely holding the little creature in your hand can be fatal.

The following Florida toads and frogs have the most irritating skin secretions: Marine or Giant Toad, Eastern Spadefoot Toad, Cuban Treefrog, and River Frog. It is a good idea to wash well after handling one of these creatures.

△ The sausage-shaped throat pouch of the Oak Toad is perhaps the largest pouch of any toad in Florida (in relation to the toad's size). The pouch is used in producing the toad's high-volume call. The Oak Toad is Florida's smallest toad, barely over one inch in length!

Marine Toad

Marine Toad or Giant Toad

This big toad was introduced into Florida many years ago. Originally it ranged from south Texas to southern South America. It has been described as "the most introduced amphibian in the world." It eats certain beetles that damage sugarcane and may have been brought into Florida for this reason. It is usually a rusty or orange-brown color.

This toad produces a milky secretion in its parotid glands that is quite toxic and can sicken or even kill a dog or cat unlucky enough to bite into one. If you handle this toad, wash your hands carefully afterwards. Do not get the secretions from its skin into your eyes or mouth! Nevertheless, it makes a good terrarium pet and is one of the few toads or frogs in the world willing to eat cat or dog food as well as insects.

Bufo marinus. Range in Florida: south Florida, the Keys, and the Tampa area. Maximum length: 9 inches.

△ Note the large number of mosquitos dining on this toad. Yes! Like humans, toads also have blood, as can be seen from the engorged mosquitos on the toad's hind limbs and nose. The photographer was not too comfortable either.

△ Most toads are quite variable in color as seen in these photos. Note the toxic milky secretions on this Giant Toad.

INSTANT SUNTAN

The skin of frogs is somewhat transparent and has a layer of dark pigment cells below the surface. These cells contract and expand automatically in response to changes in the frog's environment such as light, heat, and the color of its surroundings as sensed by the frog's eyes. When the dark pigment cells expand, the frog becomes a darker color. Cold, damp weather disperses the pigment in the skins of frogs and makes the frogs darker, thus capable of absorbing more heat from sunlight. Warm weather concentrates the dark pigments making the frogs paler, and more capable of reflecting sunlight, thus keeping them cooler on hot days.

Some researchers believe that these color changes are not strictly controlled by reflex but that frogs can produce color changes at will.

This photo shows how very large the Giant Toad can become, although most specimens are not this big.

Bullfrog

This is the most famous frog in the U.S., not only because of its great size but also because its hind legs are considered a delicacy by many. (Most frog legs sold in Florida, however, are those of Pig Frogs.) It can measure up to 12 inches with its legs outstretched! It is generally dark green to brown on its upper surfaces and white or creamy underneath. Its nose is rounded, unlike the pointed snout of the Pig Frog. It lives around permanent bodies of fresh water, including lakes and ponds and the sluggish portions of creeks. It is a voracious eater and devours just about any animal that is smaller than itself. Its call is a very deep-pitched *jurrooom*. It is less aquatic than the Pig Frog and usually calls from the shore. On a still evening its call can be heard from a quarter of a mile away. The Bullfrog has been introduced into many western states where it was not originally found.

Rana catesbeiana. Range in Florida: all of North Florida south to Manatee and Hardee Counties. Maximum length: 8 inches.

BULLFROG VS. PIG FROG

I. THE VISUAL TEST ▷

This photo shows a Pig Frog and a Bullfrog together. People who have worked closely with the two species can usually tell them apart by sight. Pig Frogs have a narrower and more pointed snout and, Bullfrogs appear to be a bit stouter. Pig Frogs are also generally lighter green on their upper surfaces than Bullfrogs. However, there is so much overlap that these characteristics alone are not sufficient for positive identification.

II. THE THIGH TEST

The Pig Frog can be positively identified by the presence of a continuous light streak across the back of its thigh (see arrow). The Bullfrog has mottled markings in the same place. ▽

△ *Some frogs, when captured, flex their limbs outward and hold them stiff as shown in the photo. This is a reflex action which makes the frog larger and therefore more difficult for a predator to swallow.*

III. THE WEBBING TEST ▷

These two photos show the differences in the webbing of the hind feet of the Pig Frog and the Bullfrog. This is one of the most reliable ways to distinguish the two species. The webbing of the Pig Frog goes almost to the tip of the fourth toe, whereas in the Bullfrog it does not reach quite that far.

△ *The longest toe of the Bullfrog's hind foot extends slightly beyond the point where the webbing attaches.*

△ *The webbing between the toes of the Pig Frog extends to the tips of all the toes of its hind foot.*

The huge tympanum is an indication that this specimen is a male. The tympanum of a female Pig Frog is usually smaller than its eye. This difference between the sexes also holds true for a number of other frog species.

Pig Frog

This is Florida's second largest frog. Sometimes it is misleadingly called the "Florida Bullfrog," in honor of Florida's largest frog. It is rarely found on land, being almost entirely aquatic. It feeds extensively on crayfish. The Pig Frog gets its name from its call, which sounds like the loud, guttural grunting of a pig. The male calls while floating in the water or while sitting on a lily pad or other floating vegetation. Like the Bullfrog, the Pig Frog is often collected for its edible hind legs. Large-scale "farming" of Pig Frogs and Bullfrogs has not been very successful in Florida.

Rana grylio. Range in Florida: entire state. Maximum length: 6 inches.

THE TYMPANUM

All male frogs and toads in Florida have voices. By hearing the calls of males, females can locate them for mating. A frog's inner ear is complex and well-developed. The outer ear of frogs and toads is located behind the eye. It is called the "tympanum," a name derived from an ancient Greek word meaning drum. This outer ear is a round membrane that is very much like the stretched skin on a drum. It is larger on males than on females, and with the true frogs of the genus Rana it is especially large and conspicuous, sometimes even larger and more prominent than the bulging eye.

HARVESTING FROGS

Frog legs are a popular food item in many parts of Florida. It is the hind legs of large Bullfrogs and Pig Frogs that are usually eaten. The frogs are hunted mainly at night from boats with the aid of bright headlamps. Airboats are preferred because they are fast enough to cover large areas. When a frog is detected by the reflection of light from its eyes, the hunter closes in and spears it with a long-handled gig that has three or four barbed points. An experienced hunter hardly even slows his airboat and can collect forty or fifty frogs per hour.

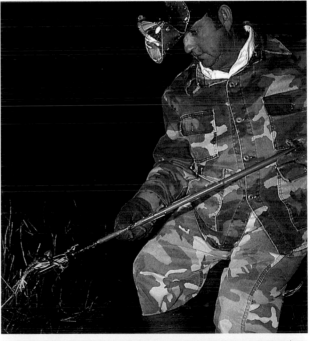

▷ **This airboat is rigged with a length of PVC pipe attached to a cloth sack. A groove cut into the pipe allows the hunter to scrape the frog off the tip of the gig and into the sack with one quick move. Brutal, but very efficient.**

SINGING IN THE RAIN
(HOW FROGS REPRODUCE)

When a heavy evening rain is impending during the spring or summer, many frogs and toads begin to call. This is the first signal of intense breeding activity. Frog and toad mating activity usually occurs at night, because darkness conceals them from sharp-eyed predators, especially wading birds. As rain starts to fall and becomes heavier, more and more frog voices are heard, until in certain wet places their choruses become almost deafening. Most frogs in Florida breed and lay their eggs in shallow, temporarily flooded ponds, ditches, and depressions. Temporary water holes do not have large resident populations of predators such as fish, salamanders and water snakes that would feed on the eggs or tadpoles, because these shallow pools usually dry up quickly.

Although sometimes it seems like frogs and toads are singing just for fun, it is the males that are calling to set up territories and to attract females. Each species has its unique call. If various species are calling simultaneously, the females can readily identify and follow the voices of their potential mates. This may seem impossible to us when we listen to the deafening cacophony of a many-voiced frog chorus on a rainy night, but with a bit of practice even a

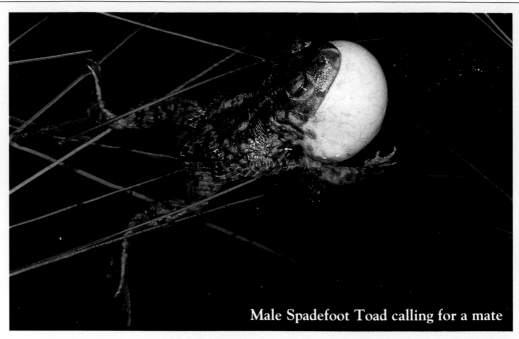

Male Spadefoot Toad calling for a mate

human can learn to zero in on an individual frog in a large chorus by isolating its voice.

A male frog or toad which is calling does not open its mouth. How does an animal so small make such a loud, continuous noise? When the male calls, the mouth and nostrils are kept tightly closed and air is shunted rapidly back and forth between the lungs and the vocal sac, an inflatable membrane

beneath the frog's throat. As air passes the vocal chords, sound is produced. The sac acts as a resonating chamber and amplifies the sound produced by the vocal chords as it transmits the vibrations to the surrounding air. Air is sent to the vocal sac rather than out the mouth because frog lungs are inefficient, and recycling the air is easier than taking a new breath.

Spadefoot Toads

FROGS MATING (AMPLEXUS)

When a female frog or toad is drawn to a male by his call, the male grabs her from behind and locks his front legs tightly around her body. This coupling of the male and female is called "amplexus."

The male frog or toad does not have a penis, so fertilization of the female's eggs has to be external. The female usually deposits her eggs in water while the male clasps her from behind. He releases sperm over the eggs as they are ejected from the female's body. The fertilized eggs hatch into tadpoles which later transform into young frogs. In many frog species, the males grow rough "nuptial pads" on their thumbs which help them grasp the slippery bodies of females during amplexus.

△ **In most frog species, the male grasps the female just behind her front legs. But in some species (such as the Spadefoot Toads shown here), the male grasps the female just in front of her rear legs.**
▷ **The female in the photo at right is laying eggs. The male covers the eggs with his sperm at this moment. The sperm may be present in this photo but not visible, because it is carried in a clear fluid which would be hard to see. The sperm must be released into the water at exactly the same moment as the eggs and very close to them, because as soon as the eggs contact the water, the protective jelly in which they are carried swells enormously into a protective mass (shown at the top of the next page). This mass would prevent the sperm from contacting the eggs. Frog eggs do not have shells and are protected only by the jelly surrounding them. This jelly mass makes the eggs float on the water's surface where they are warmed by the sun.**

Cuban Treefrogs

ALL ABOUT TADPOLES

The transition from egg to tadpole to baby frog varies with different species. The shortest larval period is that of the Spadefoot Toad, 3 to 4 weeks. Treefrogs and their kin take 6 to 8 weeks, Gopher Frogs and Leopard Frogs 10 to 12 weeks. Tadpoles of Bullfrogs of the genus Rana usually overwinter before becoming frogs.

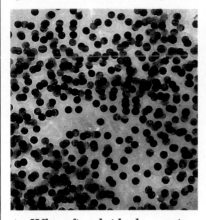

△ When first laid, the egg is a single cell.

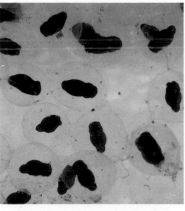

△ At 3 days, head and tail, top and bottom, are determined.

△ At 7 days, sense organs, gills and muscles have appeared.

△ At 9 days, the gills and tails are well developed.

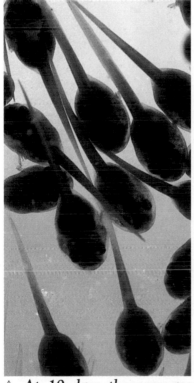

△ At 10 days the eyes are visible and the tail is whip-like.

This is the tadpole of a Bullfrog. The rows of light spots on its skin are part of its "lateral line system." This sensory system allows the tadpole to detect motion in the water caused by currents, prey and predators. The black areas of the frilly lips form a rasping beak of fingernail-like material. Tadpoles use these mouth parts to scrape up algae to eat.

△ This photo shows metamorphosis, the change from a water-breathing animal which swims with its tail to an air breathing land animal that moves about on legs. This tadpole is in the middle of its metamorphosis, with its legs just formed.

△ The metamorphosis of this Bullfrog is almost complete. In another week or so the tail will be gone and the frog will be ready for life on shore. A frog with such a tail could not hop very well. Note that the eyes are now bulging out from the top of the head.

Narrow-mouthed Frog

Eastern Narrow-mouthed Frog

Although traditionally called a toad, this common frog belongs to a mostly tropical family of frogs. It is another example of how confusing the toad/frog distinction can be. It lives on damp soil under logs and debris where it feeds mostly on termites and ants. It can be recognized by its small pointed head and chubby, smooth-skinned body. It has a unique fold of skin just behind its head, which some observers claim can be pulled down over its eyes. Its call on rainy nights sounds like a lamb bleating, one of the most commonly heard frog calls in Florida, particularly in the warmer months. It calls from deep inside grass clumps and can be very difficult to locate when it is singing.

Gastrophryne carolinensis. Range in Florida: entire state. Maximum length: 1.5 inches.

△ The color of this frog can be quite variable as shown in these photos.

◁ Note the fold of skin just behind the head of this frog.

Eastern Narrow-mouthed Frogs have been known to sit on top of ant hills and lap up the ants as they emerge.

Gopher Frog

Florida Gopher Frog

One of the nicknames for this attractive creature is White Frog. It is lavishly decorated with dark spots on its upper surfaces, but its base color is a very light gray, almost white. It is stockier than other members of the genus *Rana*. It usually does not live as close to water as do other true frogs but in dry wooded habitats where there are Gopher Tortoise burrows in which it makes its home.

It is active mainly at night. Although not really rare, it is seldom seen, especially during daylight hours. During the day it retreats into the damp burrows of Gopher Tortoises or into other cavities. Unfortunately, with the diminishing numbers of Gopher Tortoises, the Gopher Frog has been deprived of much of its favored habitat.

Gopher Frogs are best seen when they are calling from breeding ponds, which might be a mile or more from their home burrows. They breed mostly during the winter and early spring in North Florida, and later in South Florida because of the delayed onset of heavy rains. Their call sounds like a prolonged, rasping snore.

Rana capito aesopus. SPECIES OF SPECIAL CONCERN. Range: most of state except western tip of panhandle and south of Lake Okeechobee. Maximum length: 4.5 inches.

Leopard Frog

Southern Leopard Frog

This is a sleek and beautifully-spotted frog, abundant and well known for its leaping abilities. It can be recognized by a light spot in the center of the tympanum. It has been called the Grass Frog because it is frequently found resting in grasses and vegetation along the edges of fresh-water creeks and ponds. If a person walks along the edge of a pond, these frogs will leap, one after another, from the grass into the water, each one giving a squawk as it jumps three or four feet. The Southern Leopard Frog calls on rainy nights during most of the year, but it is primarily a winter breeder. It makes a variety of guttural sounds. One of its really unique calls is similar to the sound produced when you rub your finger hard over the surface of an inflated balloon. This frog will call on nights when it might seem too cool for amphibians to be out.

Rana sphenocephala. Range in Florida: entire state. Maximum length: 5 inches.

△ Note the prominent yellow spot in the middle of the tympanum (eardrum). This distinguishes the Southern Leopard Frog from other kinds of leopard frogs. Note also the gold stripe that passes through the eye, and that the upper part of the iris matches the color of this stripe. This gold upper iris is also found in Gopher Frogs.

△ This frog would eat the dragonfly on its back if given the chance. But if it turned around, the speedy dragonfly would probably escape.

△ The amount of green in leopard frogs is variable, although the basic pattern of light brown background with dark brown blotches remains the same in most specimens.

Bronze Frog

This frog is so named because of the distinctly bronze coloration on its upper surfaces. It is a handsome animal but is primarily nocturnal. During the day, it hides under rotting logs or other debris, usually close to water, but is easily "spooked" from its hiding place. The Bronze Frog seeks habitat with flowing water such as small creeks and streams. In contrast, the River Frog (described below) also needs flowing water but prefers the greater flow of water found in larger rivers.

The Bronze Frog breeds during the warmer months of the year. Its call is a strange single note that sounds very much like a plucked banjo string. Sometimes this note will be repeated several times.

Rana clamitans. Range in Florida: all of north Florida south to Volusia, Lake and Citrus Counties. Maximum length: 4 inches.

River Frog

As its name implies, this frog is found on the banks of freshwater rivers, in river swamps, and along the edges of river-connected creeks and ponds. It is common and fairly approachable. On its upper surfaces it is dark green or brown, sometimes almost black, and its skin is rough. Underneath, it is mottled mouse-gray and white. The eyes of the tadpoles are usually reddish.

Unlike other frogs, the River Frog does not wriggle and jump madly when captured but reacts by becoming limp. If you lay one down on its back, it will just stay there for a while until you go away. Its passivity is probably due to the protection it gets from a foul-smelling and apparently toxic secretion of its skin. Snakes that have been seen eating this frog became violently ill afterwards. After handling one, wash your hands well to avoid accidentally transfering its skin secretions to your eyes or mouth. Its call is a brief grunt or low-pitched snore. The tadpoles of this frog are often seen swimming in large schools.

Rana heckscheri. Range in Florida: most of north Florida south to Hillsborough County. Maximum length: 5 inches.

△ The River Frog is sometimes confused with Bullfrogs and Pig Frogs because of its large size.
▽ The bright white spots under the River Frog's jaw make positive identification relatively easy.

Bog Frog

Florida Bog Frog

On the night of July 22, 1982, Paul Moler, a senior biologist with the Florida Game and Fresh Water Fish Commission, was checking one of the swampy habitats of the Pine Barrens Treefrog on Eglin Air Force Base in the Florida panhandle. As he listened to a chorus of familiar frog calls, he began hearing some unfamiliar voices.

Sloshing into the bog with a bright headlamp, he soon spotted one of the mysterious callers at the edge of a stream. After capturing a few specimens and recording their calls, he realized that he had discovered a species of *Rana* that had never before been described.

This small frog somewhat resembles an immature Bronze Frog, but it can be distinguished by its small size and the greatly reduced webbing on its hind feet. Paul Moler describes its call as a series of 3 to 21 distinctly unmelodious chucks.

Aside from being the smallest member of the family of "true frogs," Ranidae, found in Florida, the Bog Frog is the rarest species of frog or toad in the state.

Rana okaloosae. SPECIES OF SPECIAL CONCERN. Range in Florida: found only in sphagnum bogs around several clear streams in Okaloosa and Santa Rosa Counties. Maximum length: 2 inches.

◁ The reduced webbing of the hind foot is visible here.

Greenhouse Frog

This little animal belongs to a very large family of tropical frogs found in Central and South America and the West Indies. It was introduced into Florida many years ago and is now quite common. It is brownish and has a somewhat pointed nose. It is found around homes, gardens and greenhouses as well as in moist wooded areas.

The Greenhouse Frog is unique among Florida toads and frogs because it does not pass through a free-swimming tadpole stage. The female lays her eggs not in water but inside damp rotting logs or under moist debris. Fully-developed, miniature froglets hatch directly from the eggs!

The call of the Greenhouse Frog is a soft, pleasant chirping that sounds something like a cricket. It is frequently heard around houses, often when water is sprinkled on shrubs and lawns.

Eleutherodactylus planirostris. Range in Florida: all of peninsular Florida. Maximum length: 1.25 inches.

△ The highly variable pattern of the Greenhouse Frog can be striped or mottled, but the colors remain reddish brown.

◁ The Greenhouse Frog has no tadpole stage. This tiny baby frog hatched directly from an egg, a process called "direct development."

Treefrogs

Cuban Treefrog

The now-abundant Cuban Treefrog is an introduced species that was limited to the Keys and Dade County until the late 1960s. It is spreading rapidly and extensively throughout the southern and central parts of the state. Unfortunately, it readily eats the smaller native frogs.

It adapts quickly to living around homes, and it is often seen clinging to the outside of window panes and glass doors. It can change colors quickly, from light gray or pale green to dark brown. It breeds in the warmer months, and its call is a drawnout nasal *raaaank*, usually repeated two or three times.

After a rainy night, these frogs often call intensely in the wee hours of the morning until just before sunrise. They are an abundant source of food for native aquatic snakes. Garter snakes love them, and even a captive hognose snake may depart from its main diet of toads to sample one.

The skin secretions of the Cuban Treefrog can be irritating, so it is prudent to wash well after handling one.

Osteopilus septentrionalis. Range in Florida: South Florida at least as far north as St. Petersburg. Maximum length: 5.5 inches.

△ The two photos above are of the same treefrog. It has changed its color to a much darker hue within just a few seconds. Many species of frogs have this ability.

HOW TO IDENTIFY A CUBAN TREEFROG

The adult Cuban Treefrog is larger than any other treefrog in Florida (large enough to eat the smaller species of native treefrogs), and it has extra large toe pads. It has a variable but usually mottled pattern, whereas two similar native treefrogs (the Green and the Squirrel) are more uniform in color and usually greener, but never mottled. The Cuban's skin is much wartier than the others. Note also the skin fold extending from the Cuban's eye backward above its tympanum (eardrum).

HOW TREEFROGS CLIMB

In Florida, only treefrogs have well developed toe pads. The toes of most treefrogs are expanded into large discs that can stick to smooth surfaces. They secrete mucous from the pads which enables them to stick to almost any dry surface, even if there are no protrusions to grip.

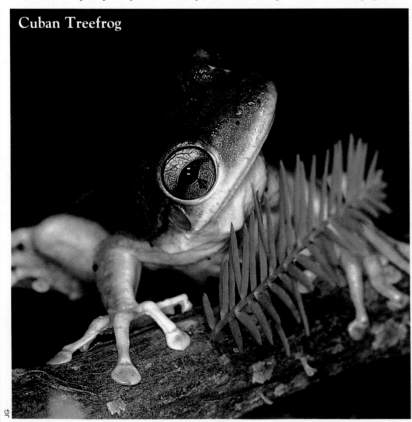

Cuban Treefrog

Cuban Treefrog on sliding glass door

The treefrogs that are often seen clinging to sliding glass doors or windows in Florida homes are usually Cuban, Green or Squirrel Treefrogs. The other species tend to stay in the woods.

Green Treefrog

This is probably the most familiar treefrog in the state, since it is common, fairly large, and adapts readily to living near homes where it searches for food around windows and outdoor lights at night.

One of its nicknames is the Cow-bell Frog because its "*quenk, quenk, quenk*" call has a ringing, bell-like quality. A chorus of many males calling together is nothing short of mind-boggling, since each one of perhaps a hundred frogs might be calling at a slightly different pitch. Their entertaining cacophany is not easily forgotten.

Green Treefrogs breed in relatively deep water (several feet) in permanent ponds, whereas most other frogs breed in the shallow temporary ponds created by heavy rains.

Hyla cinerea. Range in Florida: entire state. Maximum length: 2.5 inches.

△ Usually the Green Treefrog is vivid green, but it can change to brown quickly. The well-defined white stripe that runs the length of its side makes identification easy.

◁ This frog would dearly love to eat the damselfly on its back, but it cannot because the speedy insect would be off and away the very moment the frog turned its head.

△ Green Treefrogs often have a few yellow flecks on their backs (see photo at the top of the page). The specimen in this photo is unusual because it is covered with these markings and also because it lacks dark borders along the white stripe.

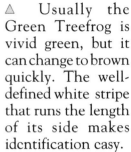

Treefrogs

Squirrel Treefrog

This attractive little treefrog can be found on vegetation around homes and gardens as well as in wooded areas. Its color varies from green to brown. Some individuals may have dark mottling on their backs. This treefrog is sometimes mistaken for a young Green Treefrog, but it has only a very weakly defined white or yellow stripe along the side. It also lacks green pigment on its all bronze tympanum. Its background color is not always green as shown in this photo but is sometimes brown.

On rainy nights during the warmer months, this frog breeds noisily in great numbers in flooded depressions and roadside ditches, often in company with Oak Toads and Pinewoods Treefrogs. Its breeding call is a loud *quonk* repeated about every two seconds. The Squirrel Treefrog gets its name from the fact that another one of its calls, the "rain call," sounds very much like the chattering of a squirrel. It is a very energetic jumper, avoiding capture by constantly leaping away.

Hyla squirella. Range in Florida: entire state. Maximum length: 1.5 inches.

Gray Treefrog

Although native to northern Florida, this attractive treefrog is often sold in South Florida pet stores. Its background color can vary from off-white to dark gray, and it usually has darker blotches on its head and back that are enclosed by thin black lines. When resting on the gray bark of a tree, it is extremely well camouflaged.

Hyla chrysoscelis. Range in Florida: north Florida south to Marion and Sumter Counties. Maximum length: 2.25 inches.

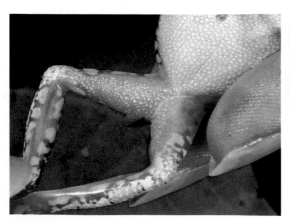

◁ The Gray Treefrog can be positively identified by the orange coloration on the undersurfaces of its legs and groin, not generally visible when the creature is at rest. Its skin is unusually warty or rough for a treefrog. In Florida it breeds during the warmer months and can be found on vegetation near hardwood swamps. Its call is a loud, resonating trill. Its skin secretions can irritate human eyes.

70

Barking Treefrog

This is Florida's largest native treefrog. It is plumper than all the other treefrogs, and it is the most endearing when you get to know it. It is occasionally kept as a pet, thriving on a diet of assorted bugs, including crickets. In the wild, it is not seen as often as it is heard.

Hyla gratiosa. Range in Florida: entire state north of Lake Okeechobee. Maximum length: 2.75 inches.

Each Barking Treefrog seems to be marked differently, but almost all of them are green with large dark spots on their backs.

◁ If you stroke the back of a male with moist fingers, he will usually inflate his throat pouch and make his barking sound. This call is indeed dog-like, and a group of males calling together on a rainy night sounds like a pack of bellowing hounds.

Eyes bigger than its stomach

△ Most of the creatures in this book eat each other, depending upon which is larger or hungrier. However, lizards (the prey shown here) are not the typical meal of the Barking Treefrog. Its usual fare consists of insects.

▷ Like other treefrogs, this species can change color from light green to dark brown very quickly, depending on the color of the place where it is sitting (and its mood). Cooler temperatures also make it become dark

71

Treefrogs

Pinewoods Treefrog

Of all the smaller treefrogs in Florida, this one is the most difficult to identify positively at first glance. It is found in a variety of wooded habitats but mostly around pine woods. It can be found high in trees or resting on vegetation near the ground. If it is sitting on a green leaf, it is usually green, often with a golden hue. However, it might also be gray.

Its call sounds like a rapid telegraph signal. On a rainy night, a group of males calling together sounds like dozens of automated office machines running full blast.

Hyla femoralis. Range in Florida: entire state. Maximum length: 1.5 inches.

Dark phase

△ This frog is most often confused with the Squirrel Treefrog. The only way to positively identify it is by a row of small, yellowish spots that show up against a dark background on the back of its thigh. (You have to stretch out its hind leg to see the spots.)

△ When resting on pine bark or another dark background, the Pinewoods Treefrog turns chocolate brown and usually reveals darker blotches on its head and back. Some individuals have a distinct dark band running through the eyes.

HOW FROGS FEED

Most frogs feed by flicking out their sticky-tipped tongues to capture insects. However, the way this works is a bit different from what might be expected. Unlike human tongues, the tongues of most frogs are attached at the front of the mouth and are free at the back. When the tongue leaves the mouth, the sticky upper surface flips over to become the bottom of the tongue. It comes down on the insect like a big, sticky flyswatter. When the tongue is retracted back into the mouth, the prey is then on the top of the tongue for easy handling.

Pine Barrens Treefrog

This is the rarest treefrog in Florida and is regarded by many as the prettiest. It is basically green, with a purplish stripe that extends from its nostril through the eye and along each side to the thigh. About the only way to find one is by following a male's call during the breeding season, March through early September. The call is a nasal *wank* repeated about once a second.

This beautiful frog undoubtedly had a more extensive range in earlier times, but now it is found only in the Pine Barrens of New Jersey and in isolated colonies in the Carolinas, Georgia, extreme southern Alabama and adjacent northwest Florida. Although this species has been known for over 150 years, it was not found in Florida until 1970. It was probably never previously noticed here because its limited habitat had been little studied by herpetologists. It survives fairly well except when one of its special habitats is destroyed by development.

Hyla andersonii. SPECIES OF SPECIAL CONCERN. Range in Florida: acid seepage bogs in Santa Rosa, Okaloosa, Walton and Holmes Counties in the panhandle. Maximum length: 2 inches.

◁ The Pine Barrens Treefrog is found in bogs where pitcher plants grow. Protection of this type of habitat would protect not only these frogs but also at least two endangered species of pitcher plants.

Male Pine Barrens Treefrog with mosquitos

Treefrogs

FROG OR TOAD?

How do you tell the difference between a frog and a toad? Much confusion has come from trying to make a clear distinction between the two. Both are "anurans" or tailless amphibians. Customarily, toads are those anurans that have dry, warty skin. Also, they hop, and they stay on the ground. Frogs usually have moist skin. They leap, and many, like the treefrogs, have toe-pads that enable them to climb on vegetation or man-made structures. In other parts of the world, the toad/frog distinction is more clouded. In the tropics of Asia, Africa and America, there are toads that climb trees, and there are frogs that hop or walk rather than leap.

Scientists do not make a distinction between frog and toad because the boundary line is too blurred in many cases.

Southern Spring Peeper

This abundant treefrog is orange or brownish on its upper surfaces and yellowish underneath. It usually has a dark, X-shaped mark across its back. Its species name, *crucifer*, means "with a cross." Sometimes the X is very distinct, sometimes it is an irregular blotch.

The peeper breeds during winter and early spring. It can be heard calling from low vegetation near standing water even on cold winter nights. A large chorus of peepers can be almost deafening.

The males can be located fairly easily with a flashlight by following their call. The call is a high-pitched, slurred *peep* repeated about once a second. Spring Peepers sometimes interrupt their peeping with a soft trill. During the warmer months, they live high in trees and are rarely heard or seen.

Hyla crucifer bartramiana. Range in Florida: most of north Florida south to Orange County. Maximum length: 1.25 inches.

△ The bronze color is more typical than the reddish specimens shown here.

CALL OF THE ANCIENT FROG

According to scientists, frogs have been around for about 150 million years, and they were the first vertebrate land animals to develop voices. This conclusion was made on the basis of the "otic notch," a bony structure across which the tympanum or ear drum was stretched. It is found on their fossilized skulls.

Since the most important function of a frog's ear today is to hear the calls of its own species, it is assumed that these early frogs with ears had voices which enabled them to communicate.

WHAT IS A TREEFROG?

Most treefrogs have enlarged toepads which they use for climbing around in trees. However, this is not a totally reliable way to identify a treefrog. Some Florida members of the treefrog family, such as Chorus Frogs, Little Grass Frogs, and Florida Cricket Frogs, are not strong climbers and lack large toepads. Their pads have been lost through evolutionary change. However, these species are still classified as treefrogs because of the skeletal structure of their toes.

Little Grass Frog

This tiny and attractive frog is the smallest land vertebrate in the United States. Because of its very small size, it is difficult to find until you become familiar with its quick little movements near the ground. Although classified as a treefrog, it is not found in trees.

As its name suggests, it cavorts in the low grasses that grow around the edges of shallow ponds and temporarily flooded ditches and depressions. It can be yellow, brown or reddish and has a gray stripe running through its eyes and along its sides.

Its call sounds like the wheezy trill of an insect and may be heard day or night throughout the year.

Limnaoedus ocularis. Range in Florida: entire state. Maximum length: 0.7 inch.

WHY TOADS HAVE ROUGH, WARTY SKIN

The color and texture of a toad's skin in many cases resembles the soil of the earth and provides excellent camouflage. In leaves, foliage, or bright sunlight, this same skin takes on a spotted appearance which matches the background pattern of its environment, alternating light with shadow.

BIBLICAL FROGS

The Book of Exodus gives this account of the second plague of Egypt, visited upon Pharaoh for his refusal to free the followers of Moses:

"And the Lord spoke to Moses, 'Go to Pharaoh and say to him, thus says the Lord: "Let my people go, that they may serve Me. But if you refuse to let them go, behold, I will smite all your territory with frogs.

'"So the river shall bring forth frogs abundantly, which shall go up and come into your house, into your bedchamber, on your bed, into the houses of your servants, on your people, into your ovens, and into your kneading bowls …"'

Then the Lord spoke to Moses, 'Say to Aaron, "Stretch out your hand with your rod over the streams, over the rivers, and over the ponds, and cause frogs to come up on the land of Egypt."' So Aaron stretched out his hand over the waters of Egypt, and the frogs came up and covered the land of Egypt." Exodus 8: 1-3, 5-6.

This dramatic event certainly would have been the fulfillment of a herpetologist's wildest fantasy. Amazingly, a similar event actually happened around Orlando one night in the mid-1980s. Spadefoot Toads were piled up against sliding glass doors and filled streets, roads, and driveways.

This onslaught of toads occurred because every favorable condition for breeding was present, something very rare. The weather was such that all the temporary ponds survived the dry period, and all the tadpoles turned into toads. Finally, lots of rain from a big storm encouraged all the toadlets to leave the ponds where they were born at the same time, so that many streets were covered with them.

Treefrogs

Florida Cricket Frog

This is an abundant and variably-colored little frog with long legs and a pointed snout. It is found around the margins of ponds, roadside ditches and temporarily flooded depressions. When approached, it leaps away energetically at first but soon stops to rest. If it jumps into the water, it usually swims right back to shore. Many Cricket Frogs are solidly colored, but if marked, there is a stripe down the center of the back that splits into a "Y" behind the eyes. The skin on the upper surfaces is bumpy. The underside is smooth and whitish. The Cricket Frog's call sounds like two marbles clicking together, about two clicks per second to begin with, then suddenly getting much faster. Cricket frogs call readily in the daytime as well as at night.

Acris gryllus dorsalis. Range in Florida: entire state except for the extreme western panhandle. Maximum length: 1 inch.

△ The "Y-shaped" stripe varies a lot in color. Studies have been made to see if frogs with different colored stripes have different rates of survival, but so far there have been no conclusive findings.

DISAPPEARING FROGS

During July, 1990, several hundred of the world's frog specialists got together in New Orleans to discuss a common problem. Frogs are disappearing! Researchers in Costa Rica, Australia, Southern California, Florida, and elsewhere report that they are having trouble finding the frogs that they study. They feel that the world-wide frog decline may be due to a global cause. Changes in ultra-violet radiation, increases in acid rain, the evolution of new viruses, or a combination of these factors have been proposed as possible causes. The frog biologists are less concerned with the loss of individual species than with the global extent of this phenomenon. Frogs have been around since the beginning of the age of dinosaurs. They have survived when numerous other animals have become extinct. Thus, their rapid decline today is a signal that there may be something seriously wrong with the global environment.

Ornate Chorus Frog

This gorgeous frog might have colors of green, silver, red or brown, or all of the above in the same individual! Each is colored differently, but they all have a distinctive black stripe running through the eyes. The nose is rounded rather than pointed like that of our other chorus frogs, and the body is plumper. The Ornate Chorus Frog breeds in winter, calling at night from shallow grassy ponds, ditches and cypress heads, from November through early spring. It is frequently heard in chorus with Spring Peepers. Its call, unlike the slurred peep of the peeper, is a sharp, metallic *tink*, usually repeated faster than once per second. When frightened, this frog usually does not jump very far. Often it just hunkers down. It is a burrower and is rarely seen except during its winter breeding activities.

Pseudacris ornata. Range in Florida: all of north Florida south to Lake County. Maximum length: 1.4 inches.

Green phase

The Ornate Chorus Frog has various color phases, as shown in these photos.

Brown phase

Florida Chorus Frog

This dapper little frog has a pointed nose, and its upper surfaces are gray with black spots, usually arranged in rows. Along the margin of its upper lip are several white blotches, like a broken white line. Its undersurfaces are uniformly whitish.

Although it is primarily a winter breeder, it can be heard around watery habitats, mainly at night, throughout the spring and summer. Its call is a loud, raspy trill that has often been compared to the sound produced when you run your thumb hard along the teeth of a comb. Though not easy to locate by its call, persistent searching can pay off.

Pseudacris nigrita verrucosa. Range in Florida: all of peninsular Florida. Maximum length: 1.25 inches.

Southern Chorus Frog

This subspecies is very similar in habits and appearance to the Florida Chorus Frog. It can be distinguished from the latter by an unbroken white line along the edge of its upper lip. It is found in the Florida panhandle and in most of the coastal plain of the southeastern United States.

Pseudacris nigrita nigrita. Range in Florida: panhandle and northern Florida south to Gainesville. Maximum length: 1.25 inches

◁ Notice that the Florida Chorus Frog (above) has a row of spots on its back, but in the Southern Chorus Frog (at left) the spots come together as a stripe.

Marbled Salamander

This is a very widespread and popular salamander throughout the eastern United States. It lives under damp leaves and logs, not necessarily near water. Its base color and belly are black, and it has bold white or silvery crossbands on its back. The female usually lays her eggs in rotting logs in areas that are subject to heavy rains and flooding. The larvae usually hatch several days after the nest has been inundated.

Ambystoma opacum. Range in florida: north Florida including the panhandle. Maximum length: 4.5 inches.

Mole Salamander

This is a small, stout species with a broad, depresssed head. The head and feet seem too large for the body. The Mole Salamander burrows but is often found under logs and in other damp places. Member of this species will gather in temporary ponds in early spring to reproduce.

Ambystoma talpoideum. Range in Florida: panhandle and north Florida down to the central part of the state. Maximum length: 3-4 inches.

Mole Salamander

Eastern Tiger Salamander

Florida's largest terrestrial salamander is not often seen. It is most likely to be found on rainy fall nights as it migrates to breeding ponds. It generally stays underground and is sometimes

Larva of Eastern Tiger Salamander

uncovered by agricultural plows. Although the color patterns differ, there is usually irregular black and yellowish mottling on its back and belly. Anyone deciding to keep one as a pet should be sure to put soil, sphagnum moss and a container of water (preferably rainwater) in its terrarium.

Ambystoma tigrinum tigrinum. Range in Florida: the panhandle. Maximum length: 13 inches.

INTRODUCTION TO SALAMANDERS

The word "salamander" is a general term for an entire group of creatures including newts, sirens, and amphiumas and is also the specific name of certain animals. Salamanders are amphibians that have long tails and moist skin. All salamanders must keep their skin moist because it is comparatively soft and does not protect them against loss of moisture. For this reason, they require damp environments. Even the land species are usually found in shady, wooded areas near water. Some burrow into damp ground.

With the exception of sirens and amphiumas, salamanders look basically like scaleless lizards. Country folk even call them "spring lizards" because they are often seen near springs. But unlike lizards, salamanders have neither scales nor claws, and their legs are so short that their bellies drag on the ground.

Being amphibians, most salamanders undergo metamorphosis. Unlike frogs, salamanders don't lose their tails when they change from the larval stage to adults. What would be called the "tadpole stage" in frogs is called the "larval stage" in salamanders.

Salamanders can regenerate limbs as well as tails and can even regenerate eye retinas and severed optic nerves.

Eastern Tiger Salamander

Flatwoods Salamander

As its name suggests, this salamander is found mostly in and around pine flatwoods. It is only found during and after autumn and winter rains when it makes its way in large numbers to temporary ponds, roadside ditches and other breeding sites. It can be positively identified by its black belly that has gray spots and flecks. The upper surfaces are basically gray, with numerous brown blotches.

Ambystoma cingulatum. Range in Florida: all of extreme North Florida, including the panhandle. Maximum total length: 5 inches.

LIKE A MOLE IN A HOLE

The Mole, Tiger, Marbled and Flatwoods Salamanders are members of a family known as Mole Salamanders. Mole Salamanders get their name from their habit of burrowing into the ground to stay moist. Their noses are blunt to help them dig downward where they feed on earthworms and other subterranean goodies.

Slimy Salamander

This is one of the most commonly seen salamanders in Florida, especially in the northern part of the state. Its body is bluish black, and it has a sprinkling of whitish flecks on its back and sides. It is usually found in or under decaying logs and in moist leaf litter, where it feeds on earthworms and other small invertebrates. Its most notable feature is a very sticky secretion from its skin, which can actually glue together the jaws of a predator and which, if it gets on human hands, is like a glue that has to slowly wear off. (This salamander should not be put in a container with other kinds of amphibians or reptiles.) Females lay their eggs in rotting logs, and the larvae develop completely inside the eggs. Unlike other salamanders, the hatchlings are not aquatic and look like miniatures of the adults.

Plethodon grobmani. Range in Florida: all of north Florida south to Manatee County. Maximum length: 7 inches.

Red Salamander

This bright red salamander is thought to be a mimic of a poisonous species. Just as the Scarlet Kingsnake mimics the Coral Snake, the Red Salamander mimics the eft stage of the Spotted Newt (a northern species). Red efts are very common in eastern woodlands and predators that learn to avoid them would probably avoid this species as well.

Pseudotriton ruber. Range in Florida: all of the panhandle east to the Suwanee River. Maximum total length: 6 inches.

BREATHING THROUGH THE SKIN

Lungless salamanders lose their gills when they change from the larval stage to adults. Instead of acquiring lungs then as do other terrestrial amphibians, they simply breathe through their skin and the lining in their mouths.

SALAMANDERS

Dwarf Salamander

This very small salamander has a light gray or yellowish back, dark stripes along the sides, and a yellowish belly. Its habitat includes swampy areas, shallow ponds and wet areas in hammocks. It is usually found in mats of submerged aquatic vegetation or on land under moist logs and debris.

Eurycea quadridigitata. Range in Florida; all of Florida north of Lake Okeechobee. Maximum length: 3.5 inches.

Southern Two-lined Salamander

This salamander is quite reclusive but abundant in the Florida panhandle in or along the edges of small streams where it often hides under mats of damp leaves. It is has two distinct black lines that run the length of the body. Its belly is yellowish.

Eurycea cirrigera. Range: north Florida and the panhandle. Maximum length: 4 inches.

Southern Two-lined Salamander

OUT OF THE FIRE

During the Middle Ages in Europe, salamanders were believed to have the ability to withstand fire. This idea might have derived from the fiery colors of some European salamanders or the fact that they would occasionally crawl out of a log which had been put in a fireplace and set ablaze. One European species is called the Fire Salamander.

Southern Three-lined Salamander

Southern Three-lined Salamander

The biggest differences between this and the preceding species is that this one is much larger and has a distinct, dark stripe down the middle of its back.

Eurycea longicauda guttolineata. Range in Florida: panhandle. Mamimum length: 5.5 inches.

Georgia Blind Salamander

This salamander was discovered when the first specimen appeared in a bucket from a deep well. Since its discovery, it has been found in several caves in the Florida panhandle and southern Georgia. It is a true troglodyte or cave dweller, highly adapted for life in total darkness. It has lost all its pigment as well as its eyes.

Haediotriton wallacei. Range in Florida: extreme southwest Georgia and adjacent Florida. Maximum length: 3 inches.

Newts

Peninsula Newt

This little critter can be found in most bodies of fresh water except swiftly flowing rivers. It stays below the surface most of the time but occasionally emerges to walk about for a few moments on floating vegetation. Its body color is olive green to brown above and yellow to orange below. Both the back and undersides are flecked with black spots. One way to find it is by dipping a minnow net through aquatic vegetation.

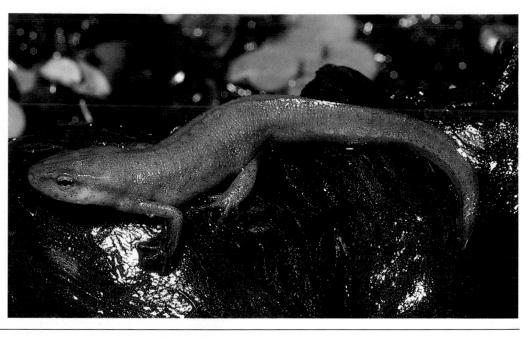

Notophthalmus viridescens piaropicola. Range in Florida: all of peninsular Florida except the extreme north. Maximum length: 5.5 inches.

Striped Newt

The gilled aquatic larva of this species transforms into a temporarily terrestrial form called an "eft" which, after a year or two on land, changes into a basically aquatic adult that usually inhabits seasonal ponds. The very attractive eft is orange-red with red stripes. The aquatic adult is brownish or greenish above and yellow below. A narrow red stripe along each side extends to the tail. Like most newts, this one eats frog eggs, among other things. This species is rarely encountered but can be locally abundant.

Notophthalmus perstriatus. Range in Florida: north peninsular Florida and the eastern panhandle. Maximum length: 3.5 inches.

EFTS: THE LAND STAGE

One of the most interesting things about newts is that their larvae transform into creatures called efts which leave the water and live on land for a year or two. The efts then transform into the adult newts which return to water and which for the rest of their lives are largely aquatic. In Florida, only the Striped Newt has efts. The one shown below has just left the water and will become brighter orange later.

SHAKESPEARE'S NEWTS

One of Shakespeare's most memorable scenes is when the witches in Macbeth are stirring up their evil brew. Among the diabolical ingredients that they throw into their pot is "eye of newt." These witches knew the finer points of potion-making, for one of the characteristics of newts that distinguishes them from other salamanders is their very toxic skin secretions. A newt ("an ewt" in old English) is a type of salamander that lives in water during both its larval and final adult stages.

The Little Newt *by David McCord*

The little newt
Is not a brute,
A fish or fowl,
A kind of owl;
He doesn't prowl
Or run or dig
Or grow too big.
He doesn't fly
Or laugh or cry—
He doesn't try.

The little newt
Is mostly mute
And grave and wise,
He has two eyes.
He lives inside,
Or likes to hide;
But after rain
He's out again
And rather red,
I should have said.

The little newt
Of great repute
Has legs, a tail,
A spotted veil.
He walks alone
From stone to stone,
From log to log,
From bog to bog,
From tree to tree,
From you to me.

The little newt
by grass or root
Is very kind
But hard to find.
His hands and feet
Are always neat:
They move across
The mildest moss.
He's very shy,
He's never spry—
Don't ask me why.

Sirens

Greater Siren

Sirens and amphiumas are large, eel-like salamanders. They are found in still-water, hyacinth-covered lakes such as Paines Prairie, near Gainesville. The Greater Siren is usually gray or olive green, and it generally has lighter green or yellowish flecks along its sides. Each leg has four toes. Near the legs, it has feathery, external gills that are usually dark red. The tip of its tail is rounded, which is one way to distinguish it from the Lesser Siren, whose tail is pointed.

The Greater Siren forages for food in bottom muck and among thick tangles of aquatic vegetation. If its watery habitat dries up, it can estivate. It seals itself in the mud and waits until rains come before resuming its activities. Unlike the amphiuma, it does not bite. It is nocturnal and is occasionally caught at night by fishermen using natural bait.

Siren lacertina. Range in Florida: entire state. Maximum length: 3 feet.

△ Notice the large, prominent external gills of this Greater Siren. These external gills are not present in amphiumas. The Greater Siren has only one pair of legs, the front ones. Although its legs are considerably larger than the tiny, vestigial legs of the amphiumas, they are still very small for a creature this size.

△ The large, exernal gills of the Greater and Lesser Siren are usually quite reddish in color.

SINGING SIRENS?

The dark and slippery aquatic creatures called sirens that are found in waterways throughout Florida bear little resemblance to the mythological sea nymphs of the same name who, by their sweet singing, lured ancient Greek sailors to destruction on the rocks surrounding their islands. As for singing, Florida sirens do croak a little bit when first handled.

Sirens are basically salamanders that got permanently stuck in the larval stage, never leaving the water as do most other amphibians. They breathe with feathery external gills that are located just behind the head, but they also have lungs, which they use extensively. Furthermore, they also breathe through their skin to some extent. They have a pair of very small front legs and no hind legs.

Amazingly, they can seal themselves in dry mud when their shallow-water habitats evaporate. Their bodies secrete a coating which hardens and protects them from loss of moisture. They emerge again with the coming of rain. Many country folk in the state call them eels.

Eastern Lesser Siren

Sirens are slimy. They produce a soap-like mucus on their skin which makes it difficult to hold a live, wiggling one with bare hands! The Lesser Siren is smaller than the Greater and has a pointed tail. It prefers to live in shallow, quiet waters that have a lot of aquatic vegetation. It often makes strange little barking sounds when it is captured or handled.

Siren intermedia. Range: mostly north Florida, south to the Caloosahatchee River. Maximum length: 26 inches.

Everglades Dwarf Siren

This is one of five dwarf sirens found in Florida. The Everglades Dwarf Siren is common in some places where water hyacinths are abundant. It lives among the roots of these plants where it searches for aquatic insects.

Everglades Dwarf Siren Pseudobranchus Striatus belli. Range: southern Florida. Maximum length: 6 inches.

Eastern Lesser Siren

△ This photo clearly shows the slender shape of the Eastern Lesser Siren. It also reveals that the siren has only one pair of legs. Compare the shape of the tails of this Eastern Lesser Siren to that of the Greater Siren shown at the top of the following page

Everglades Dwarf Siren

DWARF SIRENS

Florida has five dwarf sirens including the Narrow-striped, the Slender, the Broad-striped, the Gulf Hammock, and the Everglades Dwarf Siren. These sirens have stripes on their sides, with the Everglades Dwarf Siren having the wider stripes. The stripes of the Everglades Dwarf Siren are noticeably buff-colored.

CREATURES FROM THE BLACK LAGOON

North America and Central America have a greater variety of salamanders than the rest of the world put together. Florida has a good share of the total number of known species. Florida amphiumas and sirens are big enough and strange enough looking to seem like they might have crawled out of some primordial slime. They are the largest salamanders in the world, with the exception of the five-foot Japanese and Chinese Giant Salamanders.

△ When sirens are taken from the water, their gills fold back and are not very noticeable. This make them look more like amphiumas, since amphiumas lack external gills. However, amphiumas have two pairs of legs while sirens have only a single pair.

△ Notice in these photos the possible color variations of sirens. The above photo shows the distinctive tail shape of the Greater Siren.

Amphiumas

Two-toed Amphiuma

Also known as the Congo Ecl, this dark-colored, eel-like salamander is found in fresh water, generally living in ponds, ditches, and slow-moving streams where it forages on the bottom for worms, small fish and crustaceans. It is aquatic throughout its life.

Females lay about 150 eggs outside the water, usually in wet mud. They guard the eggs by coiling their bodies around them.

Sometimes on rainy nights an amphiuma can be seen slithering overland from one water hole to another. It has two pairs of very small, useless legs, each one terminating in two small toes. Florida also has a One-toed Amphiuma which is very similar except it is smaller and has one less toe.

Amphiumas are very slippery and should be handled only with a net or heavy gloves since they bite viciously. They are not venomous but have strong jaws.

Amphiuma means. Range in Florida: entire state. Maximum length: 40 inches.

△ Amphiumas have gill openings on each side just behind the head, but the gills are hidden inside, not external like those of sirens.

◁ This photo shows the two pairs of tiny, virtually useless legs of the amphiuma.

△ Amphiumas are found in mud and slime. They use bottom debris to hide themselves while waiting for prey such as crayfish and other small aquatic creatures.

△ These are amphiuma eggs. A grayish-pink embryo is visible inside each egg. The embryos develop around the yellow yolk. The black eye spots and circulatory systems are also visible. The eggs are held together in a mass by a sticky substance but are not otherwise connected to each other, although it might appear so in this photo.

Anoles

Green Anole

This beautiful lizard is usually seen in low foliage and on buildings and fences, rarely on the ground. The males are most conspicuous when they display their throat fans which are usually pink or gray in color. There are some isolated populations of the Green Anole in Southwest Florida which have blue or green throat fans. The lifespan of the Green Anole is two to three years.

The name "anole" is pronounced in various ways: either "uh-no'-lee," "an'-ole," or "uh-nole'." Anoles belong to the genus *Anolis*, in the same family as Iguanas. Anoles generally have slender bodies and long tails. They have long toes with adhesive toepads and claws, enabling them to climb easily on any surface, even glass. Their excellent vision helps them hunt insects. The Green Anole is the only native member of the genus in Florida. All others are recent introductions including the Cuban Brown Anole which has become abundant throughout most of the Florida peninsula.

Anolis carolinensis. Range in Florida: entire state. Maximum total length: 8 inches.

THE THROAT FAN (OR DEWLAP)

Both male and female anoles have a dewlap, but it is usually much larger in the males. It is hardly noticed when folded up but becomes prominent and flashy when extended by the lever action of muscles and bone. The dewlap is not inflated but is forced outward as the hyoid bone is stretched like a bow (see diagram). This reveals colorful scales that were hidden when the dewlap was folded. The effect is often magnified because the dewlap is transparent enough to allow some light to shine through. This is an example of bright coloration that is useful for threats, courtship, and defending territory but does not interfere with camouflage because it only appears when needed. This mechanism is common in nature.

For example, many species of birds have colorful crests of feathers on their heads which can be raised when a bright display is needed but are unseen at other times.

A particular sequence of head-bobbing and dewlap-extension displays is unique to each species and helps lizards recognize their own kind.

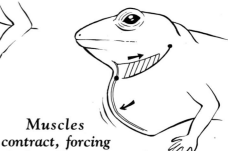

Muscles contract, forcing the hyoid bone outward like a bow.

△ This Green Anole (brown phase) is eating a cricket. Lizards do not chew their food but swallow it whole.

LIZARDS?

The word "lizard" is a catch-all term that refers to a variety of similar critters, most of which have four legs, scaly skin and long tails. It includes anoles, skinks and geckos. Unlike snakes, most lizards have eyelids that blink, tongues that are not forked, and ear openings for hearing sounds. Some lizards have extremely small legs; glass and worm lizards lack legs altogether. Among Florida's lizards, there are several distinct groups such as anoles, geckos, skinks, and the bizarre, so-called, Worm Lizard. No Florida lizards are poisonous. In fact, the only venomous lizards in the world are the Gila Monster from the southwestern United States and the related Mexican Beaded Lizard from the Pacific coast of Mexico. Lizards are mostly insect-eaters. Some species eat almost any smaller animal they can grab in their jaws, and some eat a variety of vegetable matter.

Female Green Anole
in brown phase

Before (green)

After (brown)

AN ANOLE OF A DIFFERENT COLOR

Three factors stimulate the Green Anole to change color from green to brown, or vice versa: camouflage, temperature and emotions. When an anole is on green vegetation or a light background it is usually green. As it moves onto tree bark or another dark background, it turns brown. In weather over 70°F, the anole tends to remain green most of the time. Cold weather makes it turn brown. Strangely enough, emotions also enter the picture. If two male anoles have a territorial dispute, the winner turns bright green and the loser turns brown. Green seems to be associated with positive behavior or feelings. Brown is "down." What mechanism controls the color changes? For anoles it is the hormone intermedin which is secreted into the blood by the pituitary gland. This hormone is carried by the bloodstream to special color cells where it causes changes in the concentrations of pigments. The pituitary gland is near the part of the anole's brain responsible for emotions.

THE TRUE CHAMELEON IS NOT A FLORIDIAN

Although often called a "chameleon," Florida's Green Anole is not related to the true African and Madagascan chameleons whose tails coil into spirals and whose eyeballs move independently of one another. The native Florida Green Anole acquired the label "chameleon" only because, like the true chameleon, it can change its color quickly from green to brown.

The creature shown here is Jackson's Chameleon, an example of one of the true chameleons from Africa. In Florida, Jackson's Chameleon is an import found only in pet shops.

△ Anoles shed their skin, but the old skin does not come off in one piece like that of a snake.

▷ The prominent blue eye ring disappears when the Green Anole changes its color to brown. Note the ear openings of the lizard (arrow) and the moveable eyelids, both of which which help distinguish lizards from snakes.

△ These anoles are mating in typical lizard fashion. The male is gripping the female by a fold of skin on the back of her neck. This behavior occurs in a number of lizard species and serves to prevent interruption of mating by holding the female still. Many females bear scars from these mating bites.

WAR OF THE ANOLES (GREEN VS. BROWN)

Opinions differ as to whether the Green Anole competes with the rapidly spreading Cuban Brown Anole. Although some say that it is readily eaten by the latter, this does not appear to be true. Others say that the spread of the Brown Anole lessens the pressure of predation on the Green Anole, which might be true. Many Floridians, including the authors of this book, remember that Green Anoles were a common sight around their homes until the early 1970s. Now, we see only Brown Anoles.

One explanation: Green Anoles are not prolific breeders. Brown Anoles have a higher reproductive rate, so their populations are always larger where the two species coexist. When a large number of Brown Anoles appears in an urban or suburban neighborhood, they become very conspicuous to cats because they stay on or near the ground. As cats become more adept at catching and killing the Brown Anoles, they also turn their predatory attention to the Greens that previously had eluded the cats because of their effective camouflage and because they are active higher above the ground. Eventually, the scarcer Greens are killed off while the more populous Brown Anoles survive.

It seems there are Brown Anoles wherever there are people and disturbed environments. In the countryside and in wooded areas where there are fewer cats, Green Anoles are common and are frequently seen coexisting in the same habitat with the more numerous Browns. There are still native habitats (such as the cattails around Lake Maggiori in St. Petersburg) where there are only Green Anoles, so the complete answer to this riddle may be rather complex.

Lizards like this Green Anole some-times sit on or near flowers in hopes of catching insects that the flowers attract. Some spiders do the same thing.

Many different anoles are found in the West Indies and in Central and South America. There are over 200 species! Like Florida's Green Anole, many can change color from green to brown.

87

Cuban Brown Anole

Wherever this species is found, individuals show great color variation. They generally have patterns and markings which make them easy to distinguish from even-colored Green Anoles in their brown phase.

Cuban Brown Anoles are primarily active in daylight, but sometimes they feed around lights at night. They are voracious eaters, devouring vast numbers of insects. They are themselves, in turn, a readily available food source for many native birds, snakes and other animals. Their lifespan is about three years.

Anolis sagrei sagrei. Range in Florida: most of peninsular Florida and the Keys. Maximum total length: 8.5 inches.

△ Males are frequently seen displaying the red "dewlap" under their chins. This is not only a technique for attracting a female; it also serves as a threat display for defending territory against other males.

△ Unlike snakes, lizards usually shed their skins in many pieces. Many lizards, including the Cuban Brown Anole, eat their shed skins and thus recycle the minerals contained in the skin. It is a little known fact that amphibians, along with snakes and lizards, also shed their skins .

◁ Notice the highly variable patterns on the back of this Cuban Brown Anole. Green Anoles lack these markings.

△ Mature male Brown Anoles develop crests along their backs. A lizard's crest is known as a "roach" to scientists. It is used, along with the dewlap, to impress other males competing for territory or females. The anole turns to the side to give competitors a more impressive view of his extended roach and throat fan. Together, these ornaments help the anole appear much larger.

▷ Some juveniles and female Cuban Brown Anoles have wavy lines or diamond-shaped designs along their spines.

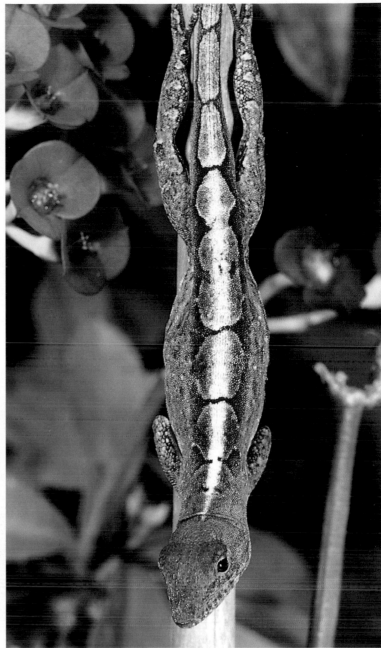

△ Young Cuban Brown Anoles sometimes have orange heads.

△ The yellow border seen on the dewlap in the above photo never occurs on the Green Anole and thus helps distinguish the Cuban Brown Anole from the Green Anole in its brown phase. The other important distinguishing feature is the even color and relative lack of markings on the Green Anoles.

The adult Cuban Brown Anoles may be gray, brown, black, or speckled. Adult males are usually darker than the females. Many males have an erectile crest on their neck and spine which they raise as a threat or when they feel stressed. Doing pushups is another threat display often performed when a person walks nearby.

BROWN TO BLACK—YES! BROWN TO GREEN—NO!

Although the Green Anole can change from green to brown, the Cuban Brown Anole cannot change from brown to green. It can, however, change from brown to very dark brown, and some individuals, especially large males, can become jet-black. Cuban Brown Anoles often show this color during territorial displays. In a garden, they can be seen sitting on elevated spots, such as the head of a water sprinkler, extending their throat pouches and looking very black, and very aggressive. But if approached, their bold, dark color will fade within seconds to dull brown. Fear or anxiety replaces bravado and they revert to a more effective camouflage color.

THE RISE OF THE BROWN ANOLE

This is an introduced species of anole that is native to the islands of the West Indies. It has been present in the Keys and Dade County for decades. In the early 1970s, Brown Anoles began appearing in many other parts of the peninsula. Entire populations seemed to show up overnight.

How did this occur? The best explanation seems to be as follows. The Brown Anole is a prolific breeder. Since the females lay their eggs mostly in low leafy vegetation, plant nurseries are a perfect habitat for successful reproduction. During the building boom of the early 70s, thousands of eggs of the Brown Anole were carried to different parts of the state in tropical landscape plants which developers purchased from nurseries near Miami and in the Keys. The Brown Anole is consequently now abundant in most of south Florida and also in many pockets in north Florida.

Anoles

Florida Bark Anole

This small anole is considered by some to be a native Floridian, but most herpetologists believe that it was introduced from the Bahamas. It is often seen on the large *Ficus* trees around Miami's Fairchild Tropical Gardens. It is quite slender and its color is gray, or brown, sometimes with a tinge of green. It spends most of its time on the trunks or limbs of trees, rarely on the ground or on man-made structures. Males have a small, yellow throat fan, or dewlap, and they engage in territorial displays by extending their dewlaps and bobbing their heads up and down. Sometimes a male will do vigorous pushups while sticking out its tongue.

Anolis distichus floridanus. Range in Florida: Dade County. Maximum total length: 5 inches.

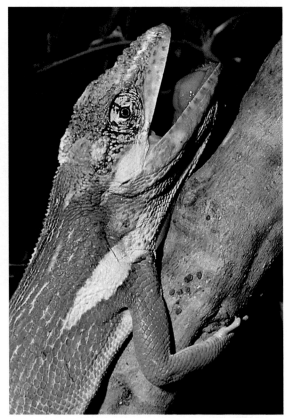

Knight Anole

This large green anole is fairly conspicuous in the Miami area, where it was introduced many years ago from Cuba. It is generally seen on the shady trunks and limbs of large trees, particularly in wooded parks and yards. It is common in the vicinity of Fairchild Tropical Gardens and in other older neighborhoods in Miami. It is relatively slow moving, but it has sharp teeth and will not hesitate to bite. In addition to eating insects, the Knight Anole also preys on other kinds of lizards.

Anolis equestris. Range in Florida: Dade and Broward Counties. Maximum total length: 19.5 inches

◁ An interesting habit of this lizard is its defensive display. When threatened, it puffs up and opens its mouth wide in a menacing gesture.

Curly-tailed Lizard or Lion Lizard

This lizard is very common in the Bahamas and some West Indian islands. It has been introduced into southeast Florida. It usually stays on the ground and is very conspicuous in gardens, on dunes, on paved sidewalks, and on low perches where it likes to bask in the sunlight. It is gray or brownish, and its tail has a slight crest of sharp-pointed scales. When approached, it curls its tail over its back like a scorpion (or a lion), and scurries into protective vegetation.

Leiocephalus carinatus. Range in Florida: parts of Miami and the West Palm Beach area. Maximum total length: 10.5 inches.

Scrub Lizard

Florida Scrub Lizard

This beautiful rough-scaled lizard is usually found in sandy, scrub habitat. This type of habitat is rapidly disappearing because it is so suitable for housing. Scrub Lizards used to be very common on Marco Island, but under threat of new habitat-protection legislation in the mid-1970s, the developers bulldozed vast areas of the island, thus limiting this species to just a few spots such as the cemetery and the lighthouse.

The Ocala National Forest is an excellent place to see Florida Scrub Lizards, either on the ground or low on the trunks of trees. They can be distinguished from their near relative, the Southern Fence Lizard, by the prominent brown line along each side. Males have a pale blue wash under the chin and on the sides of the belly.

Sceloporus woodi. Range in Florida: central Florida, north of Lake Okeechobee, to Broward County on the Atlantic Coastal Ridge, and the coastal scrub of Collier County. Maximum length: 5 inches.

Fence Lizard

Southern Fence Lizard

This common and attractive lizard is usually found on tree trunks or, as its name implies, on fences and other man-made wooden structures. Females and immature males are gray with black and white zigzag markings on the back. Adult males have dark blue on their throats and along the sides of their bellies. The upper surfaces of older males are often brownish gray or black.

Sceloporus undulatus undulatus. Range in Florida: north Florida to about halfway down the peninsula. Maximum length 7 inches.

◁ The species name, *undulatus*, refers to the undulating pattern on the backs of the females and juveniles. The adult male, lower left, lacks these markings but has vivid blue patches underneath.

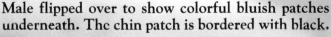

Male flipped over to show colorful bluish patches underneath. The chin patch is bordered with black.

Geckos

Reef Gecko

Reef Gecko

This common but reclusive creature is the smallest native North American lizard and probably the only native Florida gecko. Its base color is gray or brown, and it has dark lines and spots on its upper surfaces. Usually two light spots are present on its nape. In late afternoon or early morning it might be seen prowling on rocks or logs near the ground. There is a better chance of spotting one by looking under flat boards, rocks and debris in wooded areas. However, as soon as its cover is lifted, it will try to scurry out of sight. Because of the Reef Gecko's small size, speed, and elusive behavior, it is necessary to become familiar with its habits in order to see one in the wild.

Sphaerodactylus notatus. Range in Florida: extreme southeastern Florida and the Keys. Maximum length: 2.5 inches.

Ashy Gecko

This small but attractive gecko was introduced into Key West many years ago from Cuba, and it is now very common in the Lower Keys. It can be easily seen at night as it searches for insects around the lights of buildings, especially on light-colored walls illuminated by bright lights which attract insects. The adults are light tan with very fine whitish stippling. The juveniles are beautifully marked with red tails and black bands that circle the head and body.

Sphaerodactylus elegans. Range in Florida: Florida Keys. Maximum length: 3.5 inches.

GECKOS

These primarily tropical lizards are mostly nocturnal or crepuscular (active around sunrise or dusk). For this reason they are not very conspicuous, except around lights at night. The name "gecko" is imitative of the cry of a particular species. The skin of some species is covered with small tubercles that look like pimples. Geckos are very quick to autotomize (drop off) their tails. Most species are quite shy, darting quickly for cover as soon as they see a person approaching.

Ashy Gecko

IN THE HEAT OF THE NIGHT

Geckos are most active in the early evening when rocks and walls are still warm from the heat of the sun.

▽ The Ashy Gecko has smooth scales while the scales of the Reef Gecko are keeled.

Indo-Pacific or House Gecko

Many well-meaning Florida home owners have released this Southeast Asian gecko in and around their houses hoping that it might help control roaches. (It generally does not eat large roaches, although it consumes smaller ones along with other insects.) It is usually seen on the walls of buildings at night, feeding near insect-attracting lights. Perhaps its most interesting feature is its unisexuality: all individuals are self-fertilizing females! This species has expanded its population in Florida faster than other geckos because it only takes one individual, not two, to start a new colony. Indo-Pacific Geckos are very wary, darting quickly behind cover when approached. They have smooth skin, unlike the pimply skin of the Mediterranean Gecko, and are tan or gray with pale spots.

Hemidactylus garnoti. Range in Florida: many scattered colonies in south and central Florida. Maximum length: 5 inches.

◁ The gecko shown at left is a male. The females don't have the yellow head. Their heads are mottled brown in color.

Yellow-headed Gecko

This is a common Central American gecko. It was introduced into Key West and Miami prior to 1939. Males are recognized by their yellowish heads and dark blue bodies. Females and juveniles are mottled gray and cream. Unlike other Florida geckos, Yellow-headed Geckos are active primarily during the day. Furthermore, they are the only Florida geckos with movable eyelids and no toe-pads.

Gonatodes fuscus. Range in Florida: parts of Miami and Key West. Maximum length: 3.5 inches.

Indo-Pacific Gecko

SACRIFICING A PIECE OF TAIL

Amazingly, many lizards can cast off their tails at will when suddenly molested or threatened. This spontaneous loss of a not-so-vital body part is called "autotomy." If a predator grabs a lizard by its tail, the tail breaks off immediately. The place where it breaks is predetermined by a weak point (like a perforation) in the vertebrae. The muscles in the tail near this crack are also arranged so they will separate neatly. Notice the muscles sticking out of the broken piece of tail. The detached tail continues to twitch, giving the predator the impression that it is holding onto a fighting animal. If a cat or another predator suddenly grabs a lizard by its neck or waist, the lizard can also shake off its tail. The severed tail continues to wiggle on the ground for a few minutes, and it might tempt the predator to release the lizard and pounce on this exciting-looking item. The tailless lizard then dashes for freedom. The lizard regrows its tail, but the new tail is usually shorter and lacks vertebrae. Skinks and geckos are especially quick to autotomize their tails, and glass lizards get their name from the fact that their tails break off unusually easily.

REGENERATION

The regenerated tail of a lizard has no bones and does not bear the stripes or other markings of the original. A newly grown tail can be dropped off again and again. The only limit is the time required to grow another tail.

Geckos

Tokay Gecko (and Others)

A number of exotic gecko species are found in Florida in small breeding colonies – including the large and colorful Asiatic Tokay Gecko (*Gecko gecko*). The exotics are mostly clustered around Miami and other cities where reptiles are imported. Colonies are started when specimens manage to escape or are intentionally released.

This Tokay Gecko is definitely big enough to eat roaches.

GECKO EYES

The very large eyes of the gecko make good use of what little light is available during the gecko's nighttime prowlings. During the day, the eye can be closed down to just a slit to reduce the harsh sunlight to manageable levels. Notice the notches in the slit which allow the eye to be closed even beyond a slit, down to just a couple of pinpoint openings. Notice also the beautiful network pattern of the iris which scientists call reticulation.

THE LIZARD NOOSE

Lizards can be captured by the simple method shown in the drawing. Although most lizards flee when a human hand is extended toward them, many will allow a stick with a noose to approach rather closely and sometimes will even snap at the string as if its motion suggested the possibility of a delicious new prey. The noose can be made of dental floss or monofilament line with a simple slip-knot at the end.

THE LIZARD WALK

A lizard moves forward by advancing diagonally opposite legs at the same time, for example, the left front and right rear legs. This sequence causes the lizard to wiggle its body from side to side as it walks or runs.

The wiggle in the lizard's walk is the forerunner of limbless motion, the undulating movement that propels snakes. It serves as

a reminder that snakes evolved from lizards or lizard-like animals. The Sand-swimming Skink is an intermediate form. This creature has limbs, but folds them out of the way and moves through sand with a snake-like undulation.

BUILT-IN WINDSHIELD WIPERS

Geckos do not have eyelids. Like snakes, the eyes of geckos are covered with transparent scales. A gecko sees the world through something like a window pane. The gecko keeps this transparent scale clear by wiping it with its tongue. The gecko shown here is a Day Gecko from Madagascar.

Dark phase

Mediterranean Gecko

As the name suggests, this gecko is native to the Mediterranean area. It was introduced into Florida years ago. It is best seen at night around insect-attracting lights. It is often called the Warty Gecko because of its pimply skin. It can change color from light gray to almost black, depending on background color. Males squeak when they are fighting. As with the Indo-Pacific Gecko, the soon-to-be-laid eggs can be seen inside the female's belly through the translucent skin.

Hemidactylus turcicus turcicus. Range in Florida: many scattered colonies throughout peninsular Florida. Maximum length: 5 inches.

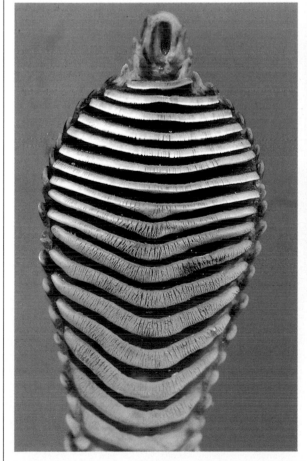

DANCING ON THE CEILING

Most geckos have extremely fine ridges and bristles on the bottom of their toes. This feature allows them to cling easily to smooth vertical surfaces, such as glass windows, by gaining footholds on microscopic bumps and indentations. They are often seen walking upside down on ceilings as they hunt insects around lights. However, their feet are not sticky. The microscopic bristles act like tiny hooks and not like suckers. For this reason, geckos cannot hold very well on wet surfaces. When moving quickly, the gecko curls the tips of its toes to release the hold on the surface before the foot is lifted.

95

Skinks

Southeastern Five-lined Skink

This is one of the most common and beautiful native lizards in Florida. It is often called the Blue-tailed Skink, but this is somewhat of a misnomer because the adults eventually become brown and lose the beautiful blue in their tails. Furthermore, several other species also have blue tails when young. This skink usually shows its five lines fairly distinctly, but older males may lose their lines and become uniformly brown . It sometimes climbs on tree trunks, but it is more often seen hunting on the ground or on man-made structures such as the wooden boardwalks found along nature trails. This creature may be poisonous if eaten by a pet.

Eumeces inexpectatus. Range in Florida: entire state. Maximum length: 8.5 inches.

Immature

Adult

THE PURPOSE OF BLUE TAILS

Blue tails may be part of a defensive strategy called deflective coloration. According to this theory, the bright color attracts predators to a part of the lizard's anatomy that is disposable. According to a conflicting theory, the blue color serves as a warning to predators that the tail is poisonous. It is not known for certain why the blue color is more prominent in the tails of hatchlings than in those of adults, but it may be that the hatchlings are more vulnerable to predation. Many Florida skinks have bright blue tails when young. Some Floridians regard all of these blue-tailed juveniles as dangerous, even referring to them as "scorpions." Actually, there is some evidence that the blue tails are poisonous if eaten.

SKINKS

Smooth, sleek and shiny are the adjectives used to describe the alert, agile and active skinks. All the species in Florida prowl on the ground for small insects, although the larger species also climb trees and wooden structures. The skink family is large and is found on all continents. Skinks are not easy to catch! Avoid grabbing them by their very fragile tails. The larger ones try to bite but rarely break the skin.

Ground Skink

This small, brown lizard is very common in natural plant communities, where it stays on the ground. It scurries quickly under leaves or debris when people approach. It is not easy to catch. It can be identified by the dark brown line that runs along each side.

Scincella laterale. Range in Florida: entire state. Maximum length: 5 inches.

◁ The Florida Sand Skink has a cylindrical body and extremely small legs with one toe on its front legs and two on the hind legs.

Florida Sand Skink

This very secretive little skink is found in sandy upland areas, particularly in scrub habitats dominated by the shrub known as Florida rosemary. It is generally pale tan. Although it spends most of its time underground, it can occasionally be found under debris or in the loose sand around pocket gopher mounds. Like a mole skink, it dives quickly under the sand when it is trying to escape a predator. It "swims" through the sand by undulating its sleek body. It feeds on beetle larvae, termites and other small insects. It is rare, and its numbers are probably dwindling.

Neoseps reynoldsi. THREATENED. Range in Florida: central peninsular Florida. Maximum length: 5 inches.

MOLE SKINKS.

These beautiful but seldom seen skinks get their name from their habit of burrowing deep into the ground in loose sand. They are usually found in dry, sandy habitats, where they can dive quickly under the sand if they are bothered. They can breathe underground because the loose, dry sand in which they burrow permits some passage of air. Some species lay their eggs in cavities as deep as six feet underground.

Bluetail Mole Skink

Bluetail Mole Skink

This subspecies maintains a blue tail throughout its life, although in some older specimens the tail becomes pinkish. It is threatened because much of its fragile habitat in central Florida is being cleared for housing and commercial development.

Eumeces egregius lividus. THREATENED. Range in Florida: highland ridge area of central Florida. Maximum length: 6.5 inches.

Peninsula Mole Skink

This sleek creature is found on coastal dunes or in sandy upland areas. It can be recognized by its brown body, reddish tail, and a yellowish stripe that extends from its nose over the eye and along each side. It is adapted for burrowing, but it can sometimes be found under palmetto fronds and around the mouths of pocket gopher burrows. It is active during the day, feeding upon insects, spiders and small crustaceans.

Eumeces egregius onocrepis Range in Florida: dry habitats in much of peninsular Florida. Maximum length: 6.5 inches.

Florida Keys Mole Skink

This beautiful subspecies can be distinguished by its brownish body, reddish tail and eight yellowish stripes running the length of its body and tail. It is very secretive but can sometimes be found underneath fallen palm and palmetto fronds on the coastal dunes in the Keys. Mole skinks get their name from their skill at burrowing, so a collector lucky enough to spot one while turning over debris must remember that it can disappear quickly into the sand.

Eumeces egregius egregius. SPECIES OF SPECIAL CONCERN. Range in Florida: Florida Keys and Dry Tortugas. Maximum length: 6.5 inches.

Broad-headed Skink

This is the largest of all Florida skinks. Early Floridians called it the Red-headed Scorpion and thought it was deadly poisonous, which is not true. Although it has five conspicuous stripes and a blue tail when young, the adult males become uniformly brown. Adults have wide heads, and the males' heads are reddish-orange. Unlike the other five-lined skinks, this species is often seen high in trees, where it feeds on insects. It will generally scurry up a tree if it feels threatened. It is active during the day and is found in high, dry pine and oak woods as well as in moist wooded areas, including cypress swamps. The bite of this large skink can hurt!

Eumeces laticeps. Range in Florida: all of north Florida including the panhandle, to about halfway down the peninsula. Maximum length: 13 inches.

Male in breeding colors.
Note the broad head.

Glass Lizards

Eastern Slender Glass Lizard

This glass lizard can be distinguished by the prominent dark stripe down the middle of its back and the several dark stripes along its sides, both above and below the lateral groove. It tends to prefer a somewhat drier habitat than the Eastern Glass Lizard.

Ophisaurus attenuatus longicaudus. Range: entire state except portions of the Everglades. Maximum length: 42 inches.

GLASS LIZARDS

"Glass snakes," as they are often called, are frequently seen in Florida. They are actually legless lizards, not snakes. Unlike snakes, they have eyelids and external ear openings. They are well known for their stiff bodies and their fragile tails that break off like glass if they are handled roughly. When the tail regenerates, it is plainly colored, lacking the stripes of the original tail. The skin of glass lizards is stiff because every scale contains a little bone called an osteoderm. Glass lizards feed mainly on crickets, grasshoppers, spiders and other invertebrates.

Glass lizards have a "lateral groove" which is a line of soft flexible scales extending lengthwise along each side of their bodies. Their bodies are so stiff that if it were not for this so-called groove, they would hardly be able to move or even expand their bodies enough to breathe. The groove is visible as a slight fold or depression.

LEGEND OF THE GLASS LIZARD

In folk legend, glass lizards were called joint snakes, supposedly able to break into many pieces and then grow back together. A Glass Lizard can actually lose its tail, and the tail will continue to wiggle as the lizard crawls away. Since the lizard might be seen later after its tail has regrown, it is easy to imagine how such a legend could arise.

◁ Unlike most other lizards, female skinks and glass lizards remain close to their eggs. Nobody knows for sure what they are doing to benefit the eggs. They might be raising the temperature of the eggs or guarding against predators. As soon as the eggs hatch, however, the baby lizards are on their own.

Eastern Glass Lizard

Eastern Glass Lizard

This is the most common of the four species of glass lizards in Florida. It is generally found in moist, grassy habitats, often around homes. It likes to burrow in loose dirt and may be found as deep as a foot underground. Unlike the Eastern Slender Glass Lizard, it does not have stripes below the groove along its side, and it does not usually have a stripe down the middle of its back. Young specimens are tan with dark stripes. This is the only Florida glass lizard that has green or bluish coloration as a large adult.

Ophisaurus ventralis. Range in Florida: entire state. Maximum length: 42 inches.

Island Glass Lizard

This is one of the least frequently seen of the four Florida species of glass lizards. It is found primarily on dunes along the coasts and inland in sandy areas, especially around former dunes. It is fairly common in the eastern Everglades. Sometimes it is found on beaches under tidal debris. Its body is usually light tan with one dark stripe down each side above the body groove, and there is often a faint stripe down the center of its back. It has more mottling along the sides of its neck than the other two species, but its most distinguishing feature is the single, broad, chocolate-brown stripe on each side.

Ophisaurus compressus. Range in Florida: all of peninsular Florida. Maximum length: 2 feet.

Racerunner

Six-lined Racerunner

This common lizard is the most conspicuous ground lizard in Florida's natural dry habitats. It is very active on hot days and is easily detected by its rustling in dry leaves. It moves fast and is quite difficult to catch, but if pursued, it eventually tires. The hatchlings have bright blue tails. This species has more stripes overall than any other Florida lizard, and its tail is very long. It is easily identified by the regular rectangular scales that cover its belly. One of its popular names is Whiptail Lizard. The males have an intense light-blue coloration underneath the head and throat.

Cnemidophorus sexlineatus. Range in Florida: entire state. Maximum length: 10.5 inches.

Worm Lizard

This weird-looking, whitish-pink lizard is an extraordinary mimic of a large earthworm. Actually, the Worm Lizard is neither lizard nor snake! It is called an *amphisbaenian*, a name that comes from the Greek language, meaning "one that goes in both directions." It is legless and has no eyes or ears. Its mouth is tucked up under its jaw, and its scales are arranged in rings around the body, giving it a segmented look. It burrows underground where it forages for termites and earthworms.

Worm lizards live in sandy upland areas and can sometimes be seen after heavy rains have saturated the ground. They are sometimes turned up during soil cultivation. Their most active period is early fall, a time when they may be seen on the surface.

Detail of head

△ Worm Lizards are underground dwellers, so they are usually noticed only when people dig in their gardens or after heavy rains, when they must come to the surface to breathe after being flooded out of their burrows. Worm Lizards use their snouts to burrow. By lifting their snouts upward, they pack sand to create tunnels. Their skulls are fairly solid and they have specialized muscles for extra power in lifting their heads. The shape of this lizard's head helps distinguish it from the earthworm.

Rhineura floridana. Range in Florida: northern peninsular Florida south to Highlands County. Maximum length: 16 inches.

Snapping Turtles

Florida Snapping Turtle

The snapper rarely basks in the sun as do most other turtles. It is usually seen while crossing roads from one body of fresh water to another. In the past, snappers were sometimes captured to eat. Because of the declining populations of Florida's herptiles, this is no longer a good idea.

Chelydra serpentina osceola. Range in Florida: all of peninsular Florida. Maximum size: 19 inches, 35 pounds.

▽ Notice the "barbels" extending out from all sides of the neck. These fleshy nodes have a sensory function.

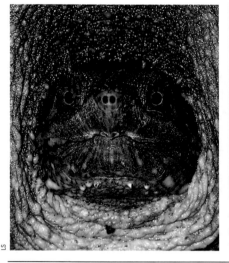

△ When the snapper is crawling, its long tail extends straight out to the rear, but when molested, it generally bends its tail forward and holds it tight against the side of its shell.

△ The Florida Snapping Turtle can be recognized by the three saw-toothed ridges running lengthwise down the top of its tail. Underwater, snappers are generally inoffensive, but on land they will try repeatedly to bite if molested or approached closely. Their necks are quite long, and they can snap and bite like lightning. Even a small snapper can inflict a painful wound with its hooked beak. When handling one, pick it up by its tail and keep the plastron (belly side of the shell) toward your body.

Alligator Snapping Turtle

This is one of the largest freshwater turtles in the world. It is found only in rivers and large streams. It can be distinguished by its very large head and the three prominent knobby ridges along its back. Although an Alligator Snapper can seriously wound a human, this species is not nearly as quick, aggressive or ill-tempered as the Florida Snapping Turtle. Nevertheless, no one should be foolish enough to underestimate the strength of its powerful jaws. A large Alligator Snapper can easily sever a few human fingers with a single bite. Amateurs should not try to handle large specimens of Alligator Snappers.

Macroclemys temmincki. SPECIES OF SPECIAL CONCERN. Range in Florida: the panhandle, mainly in the largest river drainages, east to the Suwannee River. Maximum size: 29 inches and over 200 pounds.

Young Alligator Snapper

◁ The Alligator Snapper has a unique manner of feeding. During the daytime, when there is sufficient light underwater, it will open its mouth and wiggle a reddish worm-like growth on its tongue as a lure to attract small fish. When a fish comes close to investigate, the turtle suddenly snaps it up in its powerful jaws. As the turtle grows older, it relies less and less on its tongue lure. At night, Alligator Snappers feed by foraging on vegetation, snails, mussels and whatever occasional bits of animal flesh they can find. They even eat smaller turtles.

WILD FILE

Alligator snapping turtle

Special to The News-Press

■ **Scientific name:** *Macroclemys temminckii*

■ **Details:** Perhaps among the physically densest creatures in nature, this freshwater North American turtle resembles an underwater tank with three ridges down the back of the shell. The largest freshwater turtle in the world, it spends most of its life on the bottoms of swamps and water systems that ultimately drain into the Gulf of Mexico — from Florida and Louisiana to Alabama and Texas — where it can grow to only about a yard in length but weigh as much as 250 pounds. It also has existed in the Midwest, as far north as Illinois and as far west as Kansas, where a 430-pound alligator snapping turtle was reported in the Neosho River in 1937 — although that was not verified.

Like some other turtles, it also lives to be more than 100 years old, perhaps reaching the age of 150.

This turtle eats anything that swims into its open jaws, mostly fish, lured by its tongue, which resembles a worm and serves as bait. It sometimes eats snakes or frogs or other turtles, some water plants, and occasionally birds, dead animals, snails, clams or crawfish.

Unlike other snapping turtles, its eyes are on the sides of its head, enabling it to see everything around it, if not above and behind it. Like other snapping turtles, however, it has a hooked beak — much more pronounced than its pond-dwelling relatives — and powerful jaws.

Since it spends its time on swamp or river bottom, walking rather than swimming on the muddy floor and popping up to breathe only about every 15 or 20 minutes and the alligator snapping turtle sports a shell that often becomes obscured by algae or other growth, the turtle is almost invisible.

It is most vulnerable to predation by man (or other predators when young) when it emerges in the late spring or summer to lay eggs, some eight weeks after mating. Clutches number from eight to more than 50, and the eggs incubate in shallow ground depressions or hiding places for roughly three to four months before hatching.

Remarkably, the turtle's sex will be determined by the temperature of the egg during incubation, and the newly hatched turtle, with limited chances of survival, will mature in eight to 13 years.

■ **Sources:** www.whozoo.com; www.tortoise.org; The News-Press archives

— *Roger Williams, special to The News-Press*

Lizard sighting in Lehigh Acres

■ **Kasha DiLisio** of Towson, Md., captured this image during her visit to Florida in May 2004. The photo, which she named "Lizard Basket," was taken at her fiance's parent's home in Lehigh Acres. The picture was taken with a Fuji Finepix3800 digital camera.

Notice the small under-shell (plastron) that is common to all the snapping turtles. However, the Alligator Snapper (pictured here) obviously doesn't have as much need for a protective shell as its smaller relatives. It can take care of itself with its size and fierce bite.

Snappers are rather primitive creatures, and one primitive feature they retain is a long, armored tail.

Alligator Snappers are becoming rare because of over-harvesting. They need more legal protection.

Stinkpot Turtle

This turtle is so named because of two glands on each side of the body that emit a musky-smelling secretion when the animal is captured or disturbed. Its color is generally dark brown to black with fine yellow stripes along the head and neck. It is very aquatic, not wandering about on land as much as other Florida turtles, but often climbing as high as six feet onto the branches of trees that overhang water.

Sternotherus odoratus. Range in Florida: entire state in fresh water. Maximum length: 4.5 inches.

Note the fine yellow stripes on the head and neck

◁ On its underside, the Stinkpot seems to be more flesh than shell. The small plastron (bottom shell) is joined to the carapace (top shell) by a narrow bridge. When captured, this turtle tries to bite. However, it eventually calms down and will adjust to captivity. In the wild, it feeds on fish, crayfish, insects and carrion. In captivity, a diet of meat, lettuce and prepared turtle food suits it well. One specimen is known to have lived for 23 years in captivity.

BANNED TURTLES
In 1975, a federal law banned the sale of hatchling turtles in pet shops because they can carry a bacteria (salmonella) which is dangerous to humans.

Musk Turtle

Loggerhead Musk Turtle

The preferred habitats of this beautiful little turtle are clear, freshwater springs and spring runs. Large colonies can be found in some of the big clear springs of North Florida. The Loggerhead Musk Turtle has a habit of basking high above the water on cypress knees or protruding snags. From the front, its shell seems almost triangular, except in older individuals, and it is generally tan to brown. Its large head is grayish with black spots. For a small turtle, it can give a nasty bite. Its neck is long, so it is best to pick it up by the rear part of the shell to avoid being nipped.

Sternotherus minor minor. Range in Florida: panhandle and northern half of peninsular Florida. Maximum length: 5 inches.

△ "Logger" comes from a Scottish word meaning "block of wood." By extension, loggerhead came to mean thick-headed, clumsy, or stupid. Baby Loggerhead Musk Turtles do not have large heads like the adult shown above. The loggerhead is developed as the result of years of crushing snails.

◁ Note the triangular shape of the shell of the Loggerhead Musk Turtle when viewed from the front.

Immature

Mud Turtle

Striped Mud Turtle

This small turtle can be recognized by the three light stripes that run lengthwise down the top of its shell. Its head is also striped. It lives primarily around small, shallow bodies of water and is frequently found crossing roads and foraging in wet meadows, particularly after rainstorms. Normally it makes no attempt to bite. It eats a wide variety of food and has been given the ugly name of Cow-dung Cooter by some country folk because it is occasionally seen feeding on manure. Its existence in the Lower Keys is precarious due to land development.

Kinosternon bauri bauri. ENDANGERED IN THE LOWER KEYS. Range in Florida: all of peninsular Florida and the Keys. Maximum length: 5 inches.

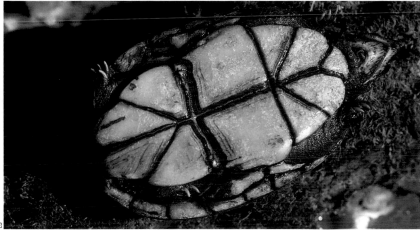

△ The Striped Mud Turtle has a hinged plastron (bottom shell), but unlike the Box Turtle which has one hinge at the front, the Striped Mud Turtle has two hinges, including one at the rear. These hinges allow the shell to be closed more tightly.

△ The Striped Mud Turtle always has two light stripes on its head which make identification easy. The three light stripes on the shell are not always present or obvious. Compare the photo above with the photo at the top of the page.

Florida Mud Turtle

This small turtle is brownish overall with faint markings on the head and no color patterns on any part of the shell. The bridge connecting the carapace to the plastron is narrow, and there are two hinges on the plastron. The hinges allow the ends of the plastron be moved to partially close the shell.

This turtle rarely wanders far away from its freshwater habitat of small creeks, drainage ditches, and marshes. The late Dr. Archie Carr, an eminent University of Florida herpetologist, reported that he once watched one using all four of its feet to dig a hole into a canal bank just below the water line. "When it was finished, the turtle emerged, turned around, and backed into the cave." Apparently they "hole up" during periods of inactivity.

Kinosternon subrubrum steindachneri. Range in Florida: peninsular Florida from Alachua County in the north to Dade County and Cape Sable in the south. Maximum length: 4.7 inches.

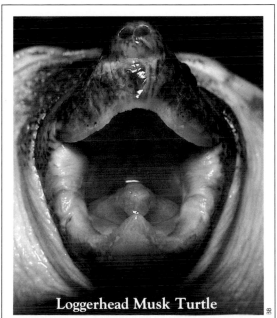

Loggerhead Musk Turtle

TURTLES HAVE NO TEETH

The earliest fossil turtles (and birds) had teeth, but no living turtle (or bird) has teeth. The turtle's hard, parrot-like beak is used for cutting and crushing (although some turtles suck their food in without chewing).

Diamondback Terrapins

Ornate Diamondback Terrapin

This particularly beautiful terrapin is now rare. The scutes on its carapace are shaped like irregular hexagons with heavy ridges forming the edges. In the center of each hexagon is a yellowish spot. The turtle's head, neck and legs are whitish gray with black spots. Its mouth has an almost comical pair of white lips.

Malaclemys terrapin macrospilota. Range in Florida: west coast from Florida Bay to the panhandle.

TURTLE, TORTOISE AND TERRAPIN

These three words have different usages in different parts of the English-speaking world. In Florida and in most of the United States, a "turtle" lives in and around fresh water, a "terrapin" lives in and around salt and brackish water but not in the open ocean, and a "tortoise" is mainly a land-dwelling creature. The large "sea turtles" live at sea.

DIAMONDBACK TERRAPINS

There are five subspecies of Diamondback Terrapins in Florida, and they all live along the coast in salt water marshes or mangrove thickets. The adults like to sun themselves on mud flats. In the past, they were plentiful. However, settlers in the state considered them such good eating that they were severely over-collected to make turtle soup. Habitat destruction along our coasts has further reduced their numbers in recent decades. Diamondbacks are adapted for living in and around salt water, and they have special glands near the eyes that secrete excess salt. They are active during the day, eating mostly small marine invertebrates, especially mollusks. In the spring, females lay their eggs in cavities that are dug into dry sand above the high tide line.

△ Baby Diamondback Terrapins usually hatch with a series of small knobs down their backs. In some subspecies these knobs remain obvious in the adults, in others they are lost.

Florida East Coast Diamondback Terrapin

This subspecies of Diamondback Terrapin has scutes which lack the light-colored spots that are so prominent on the Ornate Diamondback Terrapin.

Malaclemys terrapin tequesta. Range in Florida: east coast from Dade County north to Flagler County.

Hatchling

TURTLE SHELLS

The shell is a living part of a turtle. The turtle's backbone is fused to the inside of its upper shell, which is called the carapace. The bottom part of the turtle's shell is called the plastron. The carapace and the plastron are connected at the sides by a pair of "bridges." The specimen shown here has had the plastron cut off at the bridges. Notice that the pelvis and shoulder blades are enclosed by the shell.

Both the carapace and the plastron of hard-shelled turtles are made up of a number of bony plates covered by scales, or "scutes." As most turtles grow, each scute will periodically slough off a paper-thin outer layer, including whatever moss or algae is growing on top of it. Unlike a snake that sheds its skin all at once when it reaches a new growth stage, a turtle sheds the thin outer layers of its scutes one at a time over a period of several weeks. (Gopher Tortoises and the soft-shelled turtles do not shed these outer layers of their shells.)

With some turtles and tortoises that have an annual inactive period, it is sometimes possible to tell their age from the concentric growth rings on each scute, each ring representing a year of growth. In old turtles, however, the rings are too crowded to count accurately, or in some cases they are worn smooth.

This view of a turtle skeleton shows that the backbone is actually part of the upper shell. The lower part of the shell (plastron) has been removed.

TURTLE NECKS

The turtle's neck consists of eight vertebrae which give it great flexibility and allow it to fold back inside its shell as shown in this photo.

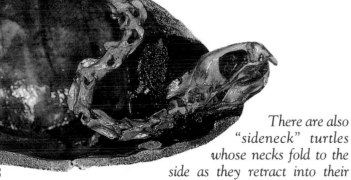

There are also "sideneck" turtles whose necks fold to the side as they retract into their shells. However, sideneck turtles are not found in Florida.

NUDIST BEACH

OUT OF THE SHELL?

Since a turtle's shell is partly formed by its backbone and ribs, a turtle cannot actually run out of its shell, as frequently happens in animated cartoons. And, because they are also fused to the shell, a turtles rib's cannot expand and contract (like human ribs) to pump air into its lungs. A turtle breathes by using the muscles that move its head and legs.

Cooters

Suwannee Cooter

This turtle is found mostly in the drainage areas of rivers that feed into the Gulf of Mexico. It adapts readily to changes in water salinity. The Suwannee Cooter's carapace is often boldly reticulated with yellow markings, and its plastron is yellow with dark markings. Its head and front feet have yellow stripes. It often basks above the water on logs or snags. It has traditionally been collected for food, which has led to a greatly reduced population.

Pseudemys concinna suwanniensis. SPECIES OF SPECIAL CONCERN. Range in Florida: west peninsular Florida from Hillsborough County to Gulf County in the panhandle. Maximum length: 17 inches.

Peninsula Cooter

This is one of the most common and conspicuous turtles in the state. It likes to bask on banks and logs, and it drops quickly into the water when approached. One way to distinguish it from other species is by the hairpin-shaped yellow markings on the top of its extended head and neck. This turtle is often seen wandering across roads as it moves from one body of water to another. Its carapace is usually uniformly dark with a pattern of parallel yellow lines stretching out toward the sides.

Pseudemys floridana peninsularis. Range in Florida: most of peninsular Florida. Maximum length: 16 inches.

△ Highly aquatic turtles like this Peninsula Cooter have streamlined shells tht allow them to swim very fast.

▷ The distinctive hairpin-shaped yellow markings on the extended head and neck of the Peninsula Cooter.

COOTERS

The word "cooter" has been used traditionally by country folk in the Southeastern United States and Florida to refer to certain hard-shelled, freshwater turtles. This word may have originated with African slaves brought from the Congo where "kuta" means turtle in the languages of a number of different tribes. Among blacks on some Caribbean islands, to "coot" means to copulate, possibly because sea turtles are frequently seen mating in the shallow waters close to shore before the female comes in to lay her eggs.

One of the most fascinating courtship rituals of cooters, as well as Red-bellied, Red-eared and Yellow-bellied Turtles, is the male's habit of swimming backward in front of the female while stroking or tapping her face with the long nails on his front feet.

Red-bellied Turtle

Florida Red-bellied Turtle

As its name suggests, this turtle's plastron is usually colored orange to red. The carapace of most individuals has one large, dark red band across each scute. In older specimens the red coloration on the back is often hidden by mosses and algae that grow there. The Red-bellied Turtle can be found in freshwater ponds and particularly in marsh habitats. Males have elongated, slightly curved claws on their front feet. This species is fond of laying its eggs in alligator nest mounds.

Pseudemys nelsoni. Range in Florida: peninsular Florida. Maximum length: 14.75 inches

▷ The long nails found on males are used for courting females. The male swims backwards in front of the female and gently caresses the sides of the female's face with these nails. In addition to having longer nails, males also have longer and stouter tails.

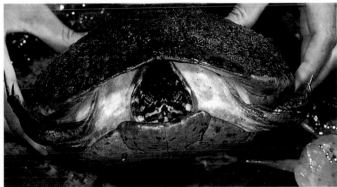

△ Notice the notch in the middle of the upper jaw. This is important in distinguishing the Red-bellied Turtle from the Peninsula Cooter. Red-bellies don't always have a red belly. Many are orange or yellow.

THE BIGGEST TURTLE EVER!!

"Archelon" means "old turtle," and the Archelon is indeed very old, about 70 million years, from the end of the age of dinosaurs. It is proof of how long sea turtles have inhabited the earth. Archelon is also very likely the largest turtle that ever lived. Although Archelon looks different from today's turtles, it does have a very close living relative, the Leatherback. This fossilized specimen was found in North Dakota in 1895 and is now on display at Yale University. It is the only complete specimen of Archelon in existence. This old photo was taken before it was placed behind glass.

Chicken Turtle

Florida Chicken Turtle

This common turtle is often confused with the Peninsula Cooter, but it grows to only about half the size of the cooter. It has a relatively long neck with more stripes, and usually its carapace has a net-like pattern of yellowish lines. These lines do not follow the edges of its scutes. The carapace is finely wrinkled, longer than it is wide, and wider over the hind legs than over the front legs. This turtle has a broad yellow band on its front legs, which is very conspicuous when the animal retracts into its shell. It also has yellow and black vertical stripes on its tail and hind legs. It gets its name from the fact that its meat supposedly tastes like chicken. It prefers quiet waters in which it can find its favorite food, crayfish. It is frequently seen walking about on land.

Deirochelys reticularia chrysea. Range in Florida: most of peninsular Florida. Maximum length: 10 inches.

▷ Note the broad yellow strip on the forelimbs and the vertical "striped pants" on the thighs which identify the Florida Chicken Turtle. The Yellow-bellied Slider also has "striped pants," but no other Florida turtle has both marks.

VANISHING TURTLES

Turtles and tortoises are among the animal species that have been most assaulted by man. People in many different societies have no concept whatsoever of turtle conservation. They continue to kill them for their meat, over-collect their eggs for food, and use their shells for decorative and utilitarian purposes. Many species have been exterminated in their original habitats, and many others are teetering on the brink of extinction. In Florida, the draining of wetlands, land-clearing for development, and highways with their turtle-crushing cars are taking an enormous toll on the native species.

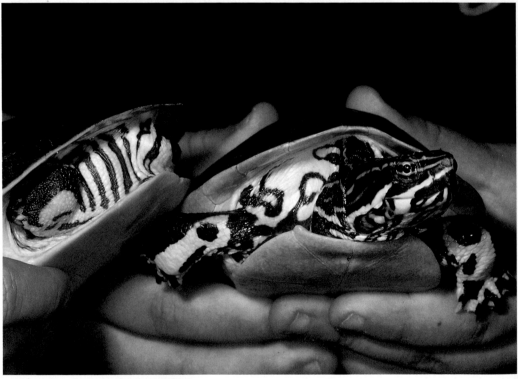

ALL ABOUT AQUATIC TURTLES

Aquatic turtles normally surface to breathe air through their lungs, but some can absorb oxygen directly from water through their skin, through the lining of the throat, or even through the lining of the cloaca (opening for excretion). Many aquatic turtles burrow into mud and hibernate to escape cold, or estivate to escape drought. Most aquatic turtles cannot close their shells like land turtles, because their plastrons are not hinged. But they can escape their enemies by diving into the water and swimming away. Most aquatic turtles are fast swimmers, and some species can outswim scuba divers with fins, as well as many species of fish. Within the United States, there is a large number of aquatic turtle species, but only five species of land turtles.

Softshell Turtles

Florida Softshell Turtle

This is a bizarre-looking turtle with an exceptionally long neck. It is a powerful swimmer and can also run on land with speed and agility. In the water, it is known to pursue and catch fish. Unlike the hard-shelled turtles, it does not periodically shed thin outer layers of its shell. The shell is soft, leathery, and pliable. This turtle is often seen crossing roads, but potential rescuers should be very careful. It can bite and claw ferociously. Notice that its scientific name includes *ferox*, which is Latin for wild and ferocious. Pick it up preferably with a net, but otherwise try to clasp the rear edge of the shell with both hands if it is not too slippery to hold.

Apalone ferox. Range in Florida: entire state. Maximum length: 24 inches.

△ Softshells get darker with age, gradually losing their patterns.

△ Soft-shelled turtles have soft lips which cover very strong jaws. Despite appearances, they can bite hard. Notice the bright colors of this hatchling soft-shelled turtle.

Baby Florida Softshell Turtle.

Spiny Softshell Turtle

The Spiny Softshell Turtle gets its name from the small spines at the edge of its shell directly behind its neck.

Softshell turtles are also called "pancake turtles" because of their flat, round shape. Their shells are soft enough to be a bit flexible at the edges and are covered with a leathery skin. As can be seen in the photo at right, sometimes the shell is so soft that the shape of the underlying bone structure is partially visible.

Softshell turtles are highly aquatic, swift in the water, and although they do bask on the shore, they usually stay close enough to the water to make a fast underwater escape if danger threatens.

Apalone spinifera. Range in Florida: St. Mary's River and Appalachicola River westward. Maximum size: 17 inches.

ADVANTAGES OF SNORKELING

All softshell turtles have long tubular snouts which allow them to "snorkel," breathing underwater by raising their long necks to the surface. This enables the turtle to stay hidden underwater for long periods. In addition, softshell turtles buried in the mud on a lake bottom and waiting for prey can breathe by raising their heads out of the mud and pumping water in and out of their throats. Skin folds in the throat are rich in blood and capable of exchanging gases. This allows the softshell turtle to remain underwater for long periods.

Pond Sliders

Red-eared Turtle

This colorful turtle was originally found from Mississippi westward, but it is now breeding abundantly in the Miami area and several other localities in Florida. It can be recognized by the bright red patches on each side of its head, hence the name Red-eared.

Trachemys scripta elegans. Range in Florida: isolated populations around the peninsula. maximum length: 11.5 inches.

Baby

△ The Red-eared has traditionally been the most popular turtle sold as a pet. When owners tire of them, they often release them into the nearest pond or river. This may account for the expanding range of the species. The release of animals into the wild in areas where they are not naturally found is not environmentally sound, since there is always the possibility that the introduced animal may prosper and multiply in its new home. The consequences are difficult to predict, but many introduced species have caused problems, especially if they take over the habitats of native species.

Yellow-bellied Slider or Yellow-bellied Turtle

This very attractive turtle was originally native to north Florida, but it is now often found in the southern part of the peninsula, where, like the Red-eared Turtle, its numbers seem to be increasing. Its rough carapace is marked with prominent yellow bars on each side, and it has a yellow patch behind each eye. Its belly is usually bright yellow and always has black blotches on the first pair of scales.

Trachemys scripta scripta. Range in Florida: most of the state: Maximum length: 11.5 inches.

△ Note the two black spots on the plastron which are characteristic of this subspecies.

MAN AND TURTLES

In addition to Aesop's famous fable about the hare and the tortoise, many other legends, myths, and customs have incorporated turtles and tortoises. One of the most colorful is the ancient cosmological legend from India that the earth rests on the back of a huge elephant that in turn is standing on the back of an even larger tortoise. Perhaps this myth derives from the fact that some of the larger turtles and tortoises can support up to 200 times their own weight on their backs! In ancient China, the tortoise figured significantly in religious tradition. The markings on its shell were believed to reveal the future to those who knew how to read the signs. In historical Japan, representations of turtles were often given as gifts, especially at weddings as a means of wishing a long life to the couple. In Thailand, temple turtles live in close proximity

△ *The turtle pond at a Chinese temple at Ipoh, West Malaysia.*

to religious shrines and are thus afforded a large measure of protection. Veneration for certain turtles extends into Malaysia, Borneo, Java and Sumatra. In Buddhism, turtles are symbols of immortality. Many temples have ponds with "sacred turtles." Buddhists sometimes attempt to attain merit by releasing these captured turtles.

Box Turtle

Florida Box Turtle

This attractive animal makes such a delightful pet that it has been severely over-collected. It can no longer be sold commercially. It spends most of its time wandering through woods, fields and gardens, but it occasionally soaks itself in water. It is usually seen after rains as it crosses roadways. Box turtles have plastrons that are hinged in the middle. This allows the animal to retract and seal itself tightly inside its shell (see photo below). Its lifespan can exceed 100 years. An Eastern Box Turtle, a close relative, found in 1953 in Rhode Island had two dates carved into its shell: 1844 and 1860!

Terrapene carolina bauri. Range in Florida: peninsular Florida and the Keys. Maximum length: 7.5 inches.

△ Note the distinctive pattern of radiating lines on this young Florida Box Turtle.

Gulf Coast Box Turtle

This is Florida's largest box turtle. Although it might have orange or yellowish markings on its carapace, it lacks the bright, radiating lines that distinguish the Florida Box Turtle. Also, it grows larger than the Florida Box Turtle. The carapace is dark brown, high-domed, and flares outward at the back. In older individuals, the carapace is almost black and the head is often whitish.

This turtle is usually seen in moist woods, often near streams. Because box turtles are most often seen when they cross highways, it might seem that they are great wanderers, but they usually spend most of their lives within the confines of an area no larger than a football field.

Terrapene carolina major. Range: Gulf coastal areas from Levy County westward to Escambia County in the panhandle. Maximum length: 8.5 inches.

△ A pair of Gulf Coast Box Turtles mating. Notice that the hind legs of the male are hooked under the edge of the female's shell. The male will try to hook its front feet as well in order to hold himself on top of the female.

HOW TURTLES AGE

The photo shows a rather aged Gulf Coast Box Turtle. However, not all turtles age in the same manner (white head, loss of pattern, etc). The turtle record for old age is 150 years.

Male   **Female**

△ This photo shows the depression in the plastron (lower shell) of a male box turtle. This depression helps a male box turtle which is attempting to mate balance its shell on top of the shell of the female. Note also the hinge in the plastron.

SAVING UP

Besides their astounding longevity of over 100 years, another fascinating fact about box turtles is that the females can store sperm and fertilize their eggs, whenever they choose to lay them, up to six years after a single mating.

Gopher Tortoise

When picked up, the Gopher Tortoise immediately pulls its head into its shell and covers most of its face with its front legs. These large front legs are flat and heavily-scaled on their exposed surfaces, making identification easy. The name Gopher Tortoise is probably a reference to the pocket gopher, a small mammal which also creates lengthy burrows. "Gophers," as they are called in Florida, were relentlessly hunted as food in earlier times. Nowadays, the high, dry ground that gophers require for their burrows is also valuable for human housing, so their habitat and numbers continue to be reduced. It is now illegal to kill, capture, own, buy or sell gophers except by special permit.

Gopherus polyphemus. SPECIES OF SPECIAL CONCERN. Range in Florida: all of the state except the wettest parts of the Everglades. Maximum length: 15 inches.

▷ Gopher Tortoise eating a cactus flower, one of its favorite foods. Cactus grows well in the dry sandy soils where Gopher Tortoises live.

Hatchling

This lovable, slow-moving tortoise is famous for digging underground burrows 10 to 35 feet long (record 47 feet) with "bedrooms" at the ends. The burrows are found in sandy, well-drained areas. In good weather, the tortoise emerges from its burrow to browse on low-growing vegetation, including leaves, grass and wild fruits. Over 70 other kinds of animals have been found using Gopher Tortoise burrows in various ways. These include burrowing owls, raccoons, opossums, gopher frogs, spiders, insects, cotton rats, indigo snakes, coachwhips and rattlesnakes. It is illegal to pour gasoline into Gopher Tortoise burrows to drive out the tortoises or any of the other occupants (see also, page 16.)

TURTLE LONGEVITY

Certain turtles and tortoises are the longest-living animals on earth. A tortoise from the Seychelles Islands in the Indian Ocean is known to have lived for over 150 years. Several Eastern Box Turtles, which are cousins of the Florida Box Turtle, have been recorded as living over 120 years. Florida's Gopher Tortoise and the sea turtles regularly live 50 years or more.

△ This photo shows the growth rings on the turtle's shell. These rings are not necessarily annual, so counting them is not always an accurate way to judge a turtle's age.

▽ A Gopher Tortoise uses its powerful, specially adapted feet to make the sand really fly when digging.

△ The elliptical burrow opening reveals the size of the resident Gopher Tortoise.

△ Detail of the foot which enables a Gopher Tortoise to excavate so efficiently.

▷ The Gopher Tortoise is one of the original inhabitants of the coastal dunes along Florida's beaches. It has been largely replaced by humans, and it is only one of many species to suffer this fate. This turtle is on top of a mound of sand excavated from its burrow. The Gopher Tortoise never stops excavating. It usually brings up some sand every time it emerges from the burrow.

Atlantic Green Turtle

This famous sea turtle is more common in the Caribbean, although it is often seen swimming off the coasts of South Florida. One of its principal nesting sites is the northeast Caribbean coast of Costa Rica.

In former times, it was a reliable source of fresh meat for sailors who visited its tropical nesting beaches. The meat of the Green Turtle is highly prized, and Green Turtles have been raised in mariculture projects for many years, particularly on Grand Cayman.

Most ecologists frown upon this practice because it encourages the continued collection of wild turtles for breeding purposes and creates new markets for turtle meat.

Chelonia mydas. ENDANGERED. Range in Florida: nests on the Atlantic coast from Volusia to Broward counties. Maximum length of shell: 5 feet.

▽ This species has a broad, oval-shaped, dark brown or olive green carapace without a ridge down the center. Note the photo at the bottom which shows that the carapace (upper shell) curves smoothly from side to side.

WANDERERS OF THE OPEN SEA

The large and graceful sea turtles spend their entire lives in the ocean. The one exception occurs when the females come ashore to lay their eggs on sandy beaches. Since the turtles use the same beaches year after year, their nesting habits can be observed by anyone with patience.

After spending a year or more wandering at sea, the hatchlings return to shallow waters to feed on marine grasses. When they are mature and ready to nest, each female probably returns to the same beach on which she was hatched! Sea turtles are air breathers, but they can stay submerged for surprisingly long periods. The record seems to be that of a Leatherback Turtle that was timed while remaining underwater 41 minutes. They can dive to depths of more than 3,000 feet. Sea turtles are famous for swimming enormous distances at sea. Some tagged individuals have been found 4,000 miles from their nesting beaches.

THE GREAT NAVIGATORS

Sea turtles migrate between their feeding areas and the beaches where they lay their eggs. These migrations may be hundreds or thousands of miles. The longest migration recorded was by a leatherback tagged in Surinam, South America, and found a few months later in Ghana, Africa, over 4,000 miles away. The loggerheads that nest in Florida migrate throughout the Caribbean, the Gulf of Mexico, and as far north as Massachusetts. But however distant their travels, sea turtles find their way back to their nesting beaches, and some tagged individuals have been recorded appearing on the same stretch of beach every few summers for over 20 years.

To achieve this feat, sea turtles must have an accurate means of navigation. The latest thinking is that they probably use more than one source of direction. They may follow coastlines when near shore, but they are also capable of finding their way across vast distances of open ocean. They may use the sun as a compass or possibly follow landmarks on the ocean floor. Some animals, such as birds and bees, are known to be sensitive to the earth's magnetic field, and it has been shown that turtles have magnetically sensitive particles in their brains. It is also possible that sea turtles smell their way across the seas by following sea currents that carry distinctive scents from far-off lands. It has been shown that

Incredible Navigators: Green Turtles which feed along the coast of South America routinely gather for nesting on the beaches of Ascension Island, which they locate across thousands of miles of trackless ocean.

their sense of smell is highly developed and that they can detect very faint odors in the water. If this is their secret, then marine pollution could have especially serious consequences for them.

Sea turtles are adapted for underwater vision in a way that makes them quite near-sighted out of water. Thus, the old theory that turtles use stars for navigation is now considered highly improbable. The magnetite found in sea turtle brains has also been found in the brains of honey bees and pigeons, two other creatures known for their homing ability. Thus, the magnetic compass method and the use of the sense of smell to detect various ocean currents are now considered the two most likely explanations of the navigational feats of sea turtles.

In any case, more research is needed to determine exactly how turtle navigation is accomplished. This kind of research is difficult because sea turtles are now so endangered. Formerly, a researcher could remove one suspected means of navigation (for example, by attaching magnets to a turtle's head to distort any magnetic sense) from half of a group of tagged turtles and see how their ability to return to their nesting beaches compared to the other half of the group. Such experiments which could endanger the lives of these increasingly rare creatures can no longer be conducted.

HOW TURTLE EXCLUDERS WORK

Hundreds of young and adult sea turtles are drowned each year by becoming entangled in shrimp nets. The new laws that require shrimpers to use "turtle excluder devices" (TEDS) on their nets are expected to reduce the death toll. All species of sea turtles world-wide are threatened with extinction, and, tragically, some are expected to be completely gone by the year 2000. The most vulnerable at this time is Kemp's Ridley, which grows up in Florida waters.

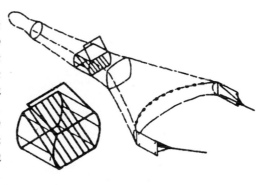

Sea turtle escaping from a shrimp net through the door of a TED

Workman/NFWS

SEA TURTLES

Loggerhead Turtle

This is the most common marine turtle that visits the Florida coasts. Adults can be recognized by their reddish-brown carapace that is elongated and heart-shaped, and by the large head and broad jaws. There are historical accounts of giant Loggerheads weighing up to 1,000 pounds. Nowadays, however, they rarely attain half that size. Like all other species of sea turtles, Loggerheads are diminishing in numbers year after year, although conservation efforts are helping to reduce these losses.

Caretta caretta. THREATENED. Range: nests on both the Atlantic and Gulf coasts. Maximum length: 4 feet.

HOW LIGHTS ON BEACHES CONFUSE SEA TURTLES

Hatchlings emerge from the sand during the night and head for the brightest horizon. If this happens to be over the water, they end up in the surf, which is normal. If the lights of a nearby city or buildings along the shore form the brightest horizon, the hatchlings head in that direction, and very few are likely to survive. Their survival rate is thus much better on shorelines that are not developed, than on beaches with brightly-lit condominiums and houses. Many beach communities have adopted ordinances to restrict beach lighting.

WHERE TO OBSERVE SEA TURTLES NESTING IN FLORIDA

Loggerheads, Green Turtles, and Leatherbacks nest on the east coast of Florida. The most dense nesting occurs on beaches between Cape Canaveral and Palm Beach. Loggerheads also nest on the west coast, particularly on Manasota and Casey Keys south of Sarasota, relatively undeveloped areas. Sarasota County alone had over 1500 nests in 1989.

Key to Map:

▬▬▬ *Loggerheads (May-August)*
Green Turtles (June -September)
Leatherbacks (March-June)

▮ ▮ ▮ *Loggerheads only (May-August)*

NESTING BEACH ETIQUETTE

1. Turtles don't like lights, so try not to use flashlights. If you must use one, partially cover the beam and keep it pointed downward. Never shine it up and down the beach or out to sea, as it can chase away turtles.

2. Find nesting turtles by walking along the edge of the water and looking for a track that appears to have been made by a small bulldozer coming out of the sea.

3. Females emerging on a nesting beach are very shy and should not be approached as they come out of the water. They might decide to retreat into the sea. Once they have finished digging their nest and start to lay eggs, they are less easily frightened. This is the time to approach for a good look. You can tell a female is at this stage when she stops moving her feet for a few minutes and sits still, breathing heavily.

4. After laying is completed, beware of a spray of sand toward the rear as the female uses her powerful flippers to cover her nest hole.

5. Sea turtles are legally protected. It is not only a bad idea to disturb nesting females, the eggs, or the hatchlings, it is also against the law.

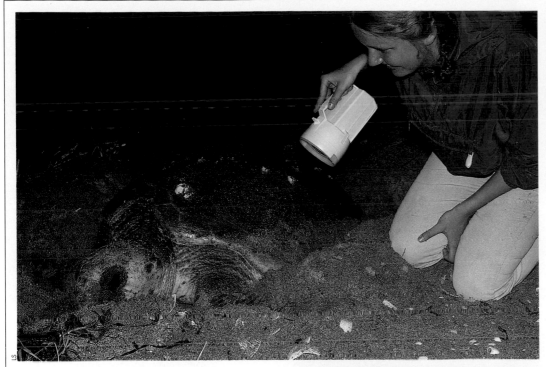

HOW SEA TURTLES NEST

In Florida, sea turtle nesting occurs in late spring and summer. The turtles mate offshore. The female comes ashore after dark and crawls to a suitable spot in soft sand, usually above the high-tide line. Using her rear feeet, she digs a cavity in the sand, 20 to 30 inches deep (much deeper for leatherbacks), into which she deposits a large number of spherical eggs. The number varies with the species. She then carefullycovers the nest hole with sand.

Once is not enough. During the nesting season, it is rare for a female to lay only one clutch of eggs. She may venture ashore from three to as many as ten times. For this reason, researchers can estimate the number of breeding turtles only roughly by counting the number of nests found on a breeding beach. All in all, a single female might deposit from 300 to 800 eggs from late spring through August. Most females wait two or three years before laying eggs again.

Even as the eggs are being laid, they are subject to intense predation. Raccoons, for example, have often been seen stealing eggs as soon as they are expelled from the mother turtle's body. Ghost crabs, armadillos and dogs also devour the eggs of sea turtles. On a world-wide scale, humans are the worst of all predators. In many parts of the world, continual nest raiding has caused serious declines in sea turtle populations. Fortunately, in Florida this illegal custom is now a thing of the past.

Newly hatched sea turtles are also preyed upon heavily. Although the tiny hatchlings emerge from their nests at night, many are caught and eaten by ghost crabs, raccoons, dogs, and night herons as they make their journey from the nest to the surf. Even those that succeeed in reaching the water are in constant danger of being eaten by fish and sharks.

△ Females may change their minds and go back into the water if conditions on the beach don't look favorable. Recently, a new hazard has appeared. With the growing interest in ecotourism, sometimes crowds of turtle-lovers line the beaches clutching cameras and flash-lights. This might be enough to deter a female. But once egg laying starts, sea turtles become single-minded and allow nothing to distract them until their task is complete, not even egg collectors, photographers, or dogs.

△ *The famous tear.* While a sea turtle lays her eggs, she continually exudes a thick fluid from her eyes. According to legend, she is crying, either in pain or over the uncertain fate of her offspring. In reality, sea turtles exude this fluid constantly, even while swimming in the sea. This is a way to help rid the kidneys of excess salt. The highly-saline fluid passes through a large gland at the rear corner of the eye. The copious flow of mucus also helps to wash sand from the turtle's eyes while it is on the beach. In addition to sea turtles, Diamondback Terrapins, which live in brackish water, also excrete excess salt through tears.

△ Baby sea turtles hatch together, and then the whole gang bursts from the nest at the same moment, thus giving predators less chance to pick them off one at a time. They tend to hatch at times when they are less vulnerable, often at night, and especially during rain. They waste no time, and are into the surf within minutes.

△ The empty nest.

△ Hatchling Loggerhead heading for the sea.

SEA TURTLES

Atlantic Hawksbill Turtle

This sea turtle rarely nests in Florida, preferring Caribbean beaches. It is often seen by divers in the Florida Keys. Its meat is eaten, and its shell has long been used to make jewelry. The continued high demand for its shell, particularly by the Japanese, could spell eventual doom for this turtle.

Eretmochelys imbricata. ENDANGERED. Range in Florida: off the south Florida coasts, particularly around coral reefs. Maximum length: 3 feet.

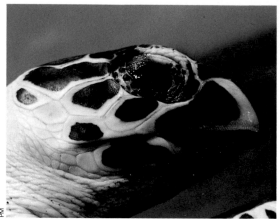

△ The turtle's snout looks likes a hawk's beak, and the dark scales on its head have yellow margins.

▷ Sea turtles swim mostly with their front flippers, in contrast to freshwater turtles that use both front and rear flippers.

△ The Atlantic Hawksbill has a carapace that is shield- or heart-shaped. It is is greenish brown and tan with the familiar "tortoise shell" mottling. The carapace is keeled down the center, and its scutes overlap except in hatchlings and older adutls.

SEA TURTLE CONSERVATION IN FLORIDA

Through the centuries, sea turtles have been used as a source of food. When European sailors began exploring the western Atlantic and Caribbean waters, they discovered an abundant supply of fresh meat and eggs wherever sea turtles were found emerging on nesting beaches. However, many colonies were destroyed because it was the reproducing females that were taken (males stay in the water and do not come up on the beach). A few countries still export turtle meat, tortoise shells, skins, oil (for cosmetics) and souvenirs. These commercial enterprises have a devastating effect where they exist.

Sea turtles in Florida have enjoyed at least partial protection since 1959. The major threats to sea turtles at present are accidental death in the nets of fishermen and shrimp trawlers, and destruction and degradation of the environment. Shrimp trawlers now use TEDS (see page 115) help to prevent the drowning of sea turtles, but other enterprises such as gill-net fishing on the East Coast of Florida still account for a substantial number of kills.

Many sea turtles suffer the same fate as manatees; they are struck by boat propellers. This danger will grow as Florida's population increases. But a greater danger is the loss in the quality of their habitat, both on the beaches and in the oceans. Plastic bags and other floating debris are sometimes eaten by sea turtles and can be fatal. Many stranded sea turtles are found to have plastic of various types in their guts, and in some cases it blocks digestion and causes death. When crude oil floats on the ocean surface, it degrades into tar and forms sticky balls which accumulate in places where juvenile turtles feed. If bitten, these tar balls can cause a small turtle's mouth to become stuck tightly shut.

Although turtles are no longer hunted on Florida beaches, their nesting habitat is being damaged or destroyed by development. Beachfront lighting is a major threat as it disorients nesting females and their hatchlings. Although many coastal cities now have lighting ordinances to protect turtles, many important nesting areas are still brightly lit. Another danger is coastal armoring—the addition of sea walls and rip-rap to prevent erosion. These structures may force turtles to nest below the high tide line where their eggs will drown.

Beach renourishment, the addition of sand where it is being washed away, may actually help if done properly (the right kind of sand, put down outside the nesting season). However, if undertaken without proper consideration of nesting requirements, it may cause further problems for sea turtles.

SEA TURTLE VS MAN-OF-WAR

Ernest Hemingway described how sea turtles avoid the long tentacles of the Portuguese man-of-war jellyfish which are armed with highly poisonous barbs:

"Nothing showed on the surface of the water but some patches of yellow, sun-bleached Sargasso weed and the purple, formalized, iridescent, gelatinous bladder of a Portuguese man-of-war floating beside the boat... The iridescent bubbles were beautiful. But they were the falsest thing in the sea and the old man loved to see the big sea turtles eating them. The turtles saw them, approached them from the front, then shut their eyes so they were completely carapaced and ate them with filaments and all." Ernest Hemingway: The Old Man and the Sea. London 1952.

Leatherback Turtle

This turtle swims great distances at sea. Its eggs are prized in some places as food, but its flesh is usually not eaten. Between 40 and 125 nests are reported each spring on the East Coast of Florida. Its major nesting areas in the Atlantic are Surinam, French Guyana, Panama and Costa Rica. St. Croix in the West Indies is also a well-studied nesting site.

The Leatherback eats jellyfish in very large quantities, but jellyfish are low in calories and much of the nourishment may come from the macroplankton trapped in the jellyfish's tentacles. Because of its smooth, soft skin, the Leatherback is not bothered by the barnacles, algae, and sucker fish which usually attach themselves to other sea turtles.

Dermochelys coriacea. ENDANGERED. Range in Florida: nests on the Atlantic coast. Maximum length: 7 feet.

△ Leatherbacks are the largest of all living turtles, with adults exceeding six feet in length. Nesting females are usually under 1,000 pounds, but the males (which do not come up on the beach) can reach 3,000 pounds. The heads and shells of Leatherbacks are not covered with scales like those of other sea turtles.

The Leatherback derives its name from its unique leathery skin. It does not have a hard outer shell. Its carapace is long and triangular and is generally black with light blue or white flecks. It has long and powerful flippers.

The Leatherback Turtle has a large number of sharp-pointed structures in its throat that point backward and aid in holding and swallowing jellyfish, a favorite food item.

◁ △ Leatherback Turtle eggs do not free-fall from the female into the nest. The females use a rear flipper like a chute to break the fall of the eggs and to guide them into the nest. None of the other sea turtle species do this. Their eggs simply drop into the nest.

Sea turtle eggs do not break easily because they are not brittle like chicken eggs. Their shells are rather rubbery and flexible.

SEA TURTLE CONSERVATION WORLDWIDE

The long-term survival of sea turtles is threatened by a complicated array of factors. CITES, the Convention on International Trade in Endangered Species, has helped limit the trade in turtle products, but several major trading countries have only recently signed the agreement. The consumption of turtle meat and eggs is still a significant threat, but it occurs largely on a local level. However, there is a large commerce in sea turtle skins for the leather industry and shells for making tortoise shell products, especially popular in Japan. Other major problems include the loss of nesting beaches and marine pollution. Coastal armoring (the building of seawalls), construction along beaches, and the installation of lighting all reduce the beaches available for nesting sites. Hatchling turtles find their food on the ocean surface up until the time they reach the size of a dinner plate. Small sea turtles are not strong swimmers. They are moved by the same ocean currents that carry and tend to concentrate pollutants such as plastic debris and tar balls from oil spills. These pollutants can choke and immobilize small sea turtles. Although sea turtles have been helped by turtle exluders on shrimp boats, they are still in danger from large fishing nets, especially the so-called drift nets. On the positive side, many organizations are now working to help save sea turtles. The proposed Archie Carr National Wildlife Refuge would protect a 20-mile stretch of beach on Florida's east coast. Floridians can make a difference by encouraging elected state and federal officials to complete the funding for this project.

△ *In Malaysia, in former years, the government leased parcels of beach frontage to turtle egg collectors. The financial success or failure of the lease depended upon the turtle's whims in choosing its nest site, as shown in this cartoon by Malaysia's premier cartoonist, Lat.*

The Malaysian government now purchases eggs from native collectors and places them in hatcheries like the one in the photo at left. Still, illegal collecting is a problem. The eggs are prized for several reasons. Sea turtles are known to live extremely long lives, so according to folklore, eating their eggs is good for longevity. Sea turtles mate for many hours at a time, so it is believed that eating their eggs improves virility. These same beliefs are prevalent in many other countries including those of Central America. In Malaysia, the Muslim religion prohibits the eating of turtle meat but not turtle eggs. However, in Mexico and Indonesia, sea turtles are slaughtered in large numbers for their meat and oil.

Sea turtles were once hunted for food in Florida, but now it is illegal to molest sea turtles in any way. It is even illegal to assist them in their march to the sea or to touch a dead turtle on the beach. This law may sound harsh, but it makes enforcement possible. The wildlife officer does not have to judge the motives of the person in possession of a turtle. The same reasoning applies to laws prohibiting the possession of eagle feathers.

△ **A sea turtle hatchery in Malaysia. The turtle eggs are collected as soon as they are layed and placed in a protected area until they are hatched. They are then escorted safely to the sea.**

TABLE OF CONTENTS